A
BASIC GUIDE
TO THE
JUST
WAR
TRADITION

A
BASIC GUIDE
TO THE
JUST
WAR
TRADITION

---★---

Christian Foundations and Practices

ERIC PATTERSON

B Baker Academic

a division of Baker Publishing Group
Grand Rapids, Michigan

© 2023 by Eric Patterson

Published by Baker Academic
a division of Baker Publishing Group
Grand Rapids, Michigan
www.bakeracademic.com

Printed in the United States of America

Library of Congress Cataloging-in-Publication Data
Names: Patterson, Eric, 1971– author.
Title: A basic guide to the just war tradition : Christian foundations and practices / Eric Patterson.
Description: Grand Rapids, Michigan : Baker Academic, a division of Baker Publishing Group, [2023] | Includes bibliographical references and index.
Identifiers: LCCN 2023014297 | ISBN 9781540965479 (paperback) | ISBN 9781540966889 (casebound) | ISBN 9781493443031 (ebook) | ISBN 9781493443048 (pdf)
Subjects: LCSH: Just war doctrine. | War—Religious aspects—Christianity.
Classification: LCC BT736.2 .P3347 2023 | DDC 241/.6242—dc23/eng/20230726
LC record available at https://lccn.loc.gov/2023014297

Baker Publishing Group publications use paper produced from sustainable forestry practices and post-consumer waste whenever possible.

23 24 25 26 27 28 29   7 6 5 4 3 2 1

For Jane

Contents

Acknowledgments

The manuscript of this book was completed on the twentieth anniversary of handing over my dissertation to the provost's office at the University of California at Santa Barbara. I am grateful to many people who have assisted and influenced me over those two decades.

When it comes to this volume, I would first like to acknowledge that there are a group of Christian thinkers who have shaped my views on the ethics of statecraft by their friendship and scholarship. Most important for me and for many others is the ever-gracious dean of just war scholars, James Turner Johnson. The table of contents bears tribute to Jim. Also among this group are the late Jean Bethke Elshtain as well as Marc LiVecche, Mark Tooley, Timothy Demy, Keith Pavlischek, George Weigel, and J. Daryl Charles.

Over the years I have been fortunate to have many opportunities to try out these ideas on students, either in the classroom or in a public presentation. In other instances, scholars have given me the opportunity to publish material. I am particularly grateful to Georgetown University's Berkley Center for Religion, Peace, and World Affairs; the Institute on Religion and Democracy; Regent University's Robertson School of Government; Reformed Theological Seminary (Washington, DC, campus); Bryan McGraw and Wheaton College; scholarly workshops hosted by Nigel Biggar, Joseph Capizzi, and

Marc LiVecche; and a writing project in 2021 with Paul Copan. In the background are lessons that I learned at the US Department of State and in the Air National Guard.

I am also grateful to a number of individuals who brought their academic, theological, military, and other expertise to reading drafts of the manuscript. Many of them have likewise been influential on my thinking, and I thank them publicly for reading the messy preliminary material that became the final product: Joseph Capizzi, Gordon Middleton, Keith Pavlischek, Mark Harris, Stephen Harris, Tony Reynozo, and Pauletta Otis. I am also grateful to Brandy Scritchfield of Baker Academic for her wise input. Four other readers were indispensable: my research assistant Abigail Lindner; my longtime researcher and copy editor Linda Waits-Kamau; my mother, Dwayla Patterson; and my wife, Jennifer Patterson. Those who know my wife know that she is an intellectual heavyweight and superior author in her own right. I am deeply grateful to Jen for listening to my ramblings over the past four years and challenging me on numerous points in her careful editing of the final manuscript.

Finally, I dedicate this book to my daughter, Jane Margaret Patterson. At this stage of life, she has decided to commit to serving in the US Army. Few people in our culture seem willing to make the big commitments to subordinate themselves to multiyear service of any type, and we are fortunate for those who do, particularly those in law enforcement and the profession of arms. Moreover, Jane has studied the just war tradition and met a number of the scholars mentioned in this book. With love and respect I dedicate this book to her, and I hope that it is a resource for her generation.

1

Just War Statecraft

The Quest for Peace

B y the end of 1933, massive swastika flags draped public buildings, and Adolf Hitler's speeches flooded the airwaves. The Nazis were in full control of Germany. Over the next few years Berlin bullied and bloodied its neighbors. Germany expanded its military presence on its border, annexed neighboring Austria, intensified Spain's brutal civil war, and initiated its diabolical anti-Jewish campaign at home. In 1938, the British prime minister appeased Hitler's demands at Munich by carving Czechoslovakia in half. Meanwhile, Berlin's Axis allies were wreaking havoc in other parts of the globe. In 1931, Japan occupied Manchuria and began to extend its brutal rule across China. Italy staged a savage invasion of Ethiopia in 1935.

Germany's *blitzkrieg* assault in Poland on September 1, 1939, officially started World War II and pulled most of Europe into the fighting. By mid-1940, half of Europe had fallen and Hitler's Luftwaffe began to bomb British civilians in London, Liverpool, Birmingham, Sheffield, Coventry, and elsewhere. This became known as "The Blitz."

1

With tanks rolling across Europe and bombs falling on British cities, Christian scholar C. S. Lewis gave a speech at Oxford entitled "Why I Am Not a Pacifist." He published the text of the speech as an essay several months later. In the midst of a world war, why would Lewis have felt the need to argue against pacifism? Was the pull toward pacifism really a risk for British people experiencing a national emergency as the Nazis attacked their homeland?

The answer is, "Yes." The Great War of 1914–18 had been so horrific and debilitating that many British citizens and politicians shrank from the horrors of another conflict with Germany, putting their trust in proclamations and treaties that purported to outlaw war. Just how destructive was the First World War? France and England together lost nearly 2 million men. The estimate of Russian losses ranges from 775,000 to 1.7 million men. Germany and Austria-Hungary together lost nearly 3 million. The United States only actively participated in World War I for one year, but during that time, America lost the equivalent of 10,000 soldiers *per month*. And these numbers do not account for millions of wounded military personnel, civilian deaths, disease and famine, and then the ravages of the Spanish flu epidemic that troops carried around the world when they returned home. Trench warfare, barbed wire, poison gas—World War I was a ghastly experience of modern, total warfare, ruining civilian property and infrastructure in addition to lives.

With the horrors of World War I still vivid in European memory twenty years later, the frantic hope not to do anything that might result in another war caused a moral paralysis. Many British leaders and citizens had become pragmatic, not principled, pacifists. Their pragmatism was rooted in fear. "War is too destructive. We simply cannot go to war again." In practice, that sentiment meant ignoring German and Japanese atrocities, looking the other way as long as their own country could stay out of the conflict. Of course, Britain soon learned it could not stay out of the war by keeping its head down. The British government's policy of appeasing Hitler during the early 1930s, far from containing his aggressive campaign within his own region, had brought the bombs to the British Isles.

Britain's moral weakness provoked Hitler's bullying, as did the worthless pieces of paper that claimed to make war "illegal." The situation also provoked moral clarity and courage among critics of Britain's policy of avoiding war at all costs. C. S. Lewis was one such critic, and he argued against pacifism at Oxford.

Lewis was not some ivory-tower academic theorizing about security without ever having to experience the conditions of war himself. He served as a lieutenant in the trenches and was severely wounded in 1918. Many of his closest friends died during the Great War. Just a few months after he was medically discharged in December 1918 he published a volume of poetry, *Spirits in Bondage*, which railed at any God that could countenance such devastation. Over the years Lewis left his atheism for the Christian faith, but he never became a pacifist. Indeed, during World War II he called the pragmatic pacifism of the 1930s that enabled Hitler "wishful thinking."[1]

For Lewis, war was not something new, a novel political condition, but rather a reality of life in a fallen world. In a previous address to Oxford students he argued, "The war creates no absolutely new situation: it simply aggravates the permanent human situation so that we can no longer ignore it. . . . Human culture has always had to exist under the shadow of something infinitely more important than itself."[2] That was the experience of Lewis and his generation. The tragedy of World War I forced an entire society to ask questions about morality, war, and peace. In Lewis's case, he concluded that we do live in a world of right and wrong, justice and injustice, and moral accountability. He continued to believe that people and governments have a duty to fight evil when it presents itself, with the practical goal of seeking peace. These actions are the day-to-day vigilance of statesmen, warriors, and public officials. At his 1940 Oxford lecture he told the students,

> It may be asked whether, faint as the hope is of abolishing war by Pacifism, there is any other hope. But the question belongs to a mode

of thought which I find quite alien to me. It consists in assuming that the great permanent miseries in human life might be curable if only we can find the right cure; and it then proceeds by elimination and concludes that whatever is left, however unlikely to prove a cure, must nevertheless do so. Hence the fanaticism of Marxists, Freudians, . . . and all the rest. But I have received no assurance that anything we can do will eradicate suffering. I think the best results are obtained by people who work quietly away at limited objectives, such as the abolition of the slave trade, or prison reform . . . or tuberculosis, not by those who think they can achieve universal justice, or health, or peace. I think the art of life consists of tackling each immediate evil as well as we can. *To avert or postpone one particular war by wise policy, or to render one particular campaign shorter by strength and skill or less terrible by mercy to the conquered and the civilians is more useful than all the proposals for universal peace that have ever been made.*[3]

In sum, because peace is a perennial aspiration of human beings and strife is always a risk in the midst of our fallen condition, balancing these realities and taking appropriate action are among the most serious challenges that a society and its leaders must address.

Throughout the 1930s many citizens asked questions about war and peace. The same kind of questions returned in the 1990s as ruthless tyrants in the Middle East and Balkans started to slaughter some of their fellow citizens and their immediate neighbors. Since 9/11 we continue to ask whether the use of force and its potential moral and physical destructiveness is legitimate. Christians, in particular, may have such questions. If Christians are called to love our neighbors, how can we support war? How could we justify violence if Christians are called to peace?

Questions like these deserve answers. Some people in the 1930s used such questions rhetorically to avoid taking responsibility in the face of Hitler's aggression. They used heady calls to peace and love to rally antiwar sentiment while avoiding serious reflection about what the moral concepts peace and neighbor-love actually require. Lewis lectured at Oxford, on BBC radio broadcasts, and across the country addressing these questions because he knew the Christian tradition has answers to these questions. Theological teaching about peace, love, and justice runs deep through Christian history. But it is not the stuff of musty library books. It requires action today.

This book is about pursuing peace based on justice in the conduct of statecraft. Statecraft is the skillful political leadership of a country, including as it relates to other countries. Effective statecraft draws on the wisdom of past experience and is buttressed by moral commitment. Christian reflection on statecraft should draw on what the Bible and theological reflection on it have taught us over the centuries about human beings living together in community. Christian thinkers offer particular wisdom about the responsibility of government to provide order and justice. That tradition is called the *just war tradition*, and its essential feature is a commitment to conducting statecraft in a way that pursues peace with justice.

Toward a Just Peace

What is peace? Standard definitions usually begin with a phrase such as "freedom from . . ." or "a state of . . ." Some define peace as freedom from disturbance, oppression, or attack, whereas others describe peace as a state of harmony, right relationships, or agreement among individuals or groups. It all sounds good, but it also sounds fuzzy. Looking at Scripture, we can discern several forms of peace. Christians are told, "Let the peace of Christ rule in your hearts" (Col. 3:15). Christians are also directed to maintain interpersonal peace: "If possible, so far as it depends on you, live peaceably with all" (Rom. 12:18). Interestingly, just four verses after "live peaceably with all," Paul shifts from the *individual's* responsibility to avoid wrathful vengeance to *government's* responsibility to bring justice to evildoers and provide security to society.

Thomas Aquinas helpfully discusses these types of peace.[4] The first is internal and, for Christians, reflects the spiritual dimension of God's grace causing wholeness (*shalom*) in our lives. Aquinas rightly notes that such peace is related to love: love of God and love of neighbor.

A second form of peace is external peace, meaning relations between individuals, relations among communities and societies, and the role that government plays in securing peace. Quoting Augustine, Aquinas speaks of this external peace as "concord." Groups of people can be in concord because they are united in the desire to preserve or advance the general common good, but they can also choose a more limited cooperation that protects a good against some evil. One vision of concord can be found in the beautiful words of the preamble to the Constitution of the United States. Note the emphasis on forming a better political union focused on justice, peace ("domestic tranquility"), and the general welfare:

> We the People of the United States, in Order to form a more perfect Union, establish Justice, insure domestic Tranquility, provide for the common defense, promote the general Welfare, and secure the Blessings of Liberty to ourselves and our Posterity, do ordain and establish this Constitution for the United States of America.

This is a robust concord, peace based on shared loves of law, justice, and collective security. It seeks this peace for all citizens, both present and future. It is a form of societal neighbor-love. The term "tranquility" goes all the way back to Augustine, who in the late fourth century called political peace in this world "the tranquility of order" (*tranquillitas ordinis*).

There are narrower forms of concord, what we would call alliances of convenience, which work toward some form of shared good. A limited treaty ("concordat") or pact, such as that between the democratic US and the Communist Soviet Union (1941–45) to fight the Nazis, is a sort of partial concord. It is a form of collaboration designed to protect each country, but it is not a truly ordered tranquility between like-minded peoples embracing the same values and virtues.

With these definitions of peace in mind, what about turning the other cheek (cf. Matt. 5:39)? Shouldn't that be the foundation for thinking about peace? Lewis rightly argued that a fallen world demands that we think about peace in terms of a responsibility to protect. Lewis told his Oxford audience, "Does anyone suppose that Our Lord's hearers understood him to mean that if a homicidal maniac, attempting to murder a third party, tried to knock me out of the way, I must stand aside and let him get his victim?"[5]

The just war tradition is actually a quest for peace. Just war statecraft, or just statecraft, is properly understood as peace-seeking not just in terms of aspiration but also in terms of constructive action. As we will see, it does so in a number of ways, first by acknowledging that political authorities are responsible for promoting the good and deterring evil. It provides guidance on appropriate, just causes for employing restrained force with right intentions. In the conduct of war, it defines limits on how force is used. Finally, at war's end, just statecraft directs policies and activities toward public order, justice, and, ultimately, conciliation.

Pearl Harbor and the Principles of Just War Statecraft

Early on the morning of December 7, 1941, the Empire of Japan launched an all-out invasion of the Pacific. One of the largest coordinated assaults in history, the attacks ranged from Singapore, Hong Kong, and the Philippines to Guam, Wake Island, and Midway Island. Within weeks it resulted in the largest British surrender in history at Singapore. In the Philippines, although General MacArthur escaped, vowing, "I will return," seventy-five thousand Allied troops surrendered and were forced on the hellish Bataan Death March.

Sunday, December 7, was declared by President Franklin D. Roosevelt (FDR) as a day of infamy that would be remembered forever. What made the attack *infamous*? It was not just the scale but the treachery. Japan's diplomats had placidly pretended that the two governments were in a period of negotiation. No one expected the evil of a sneak attack on a Sunday morning without a declaration of war.

While many people slept or were preparing for church, 353 Japanese aircraft devastated the US naval installation at Pearl Harbor. Eleven ships were sunk, with others damaged; most famously the battleship *USS Arizona* sank when its ammunition repository exploded. Over 2,403 Americans were killed. Another 1,178 were wounded.

It seems obvious that Washington had to do something. But what, exactly? Who was to do it? What were the moral and legal grounds for the response? President Roosevelt's answer presupposed the basic elements of just war statecraft. We will go into much greater detail in later chapters, but for now let's look at how Roosevelt's words and actions illustrate the basic principles of just war statecraft (see sidebar).

Just war statecraft begins with the proposition that government officials have a responsibility to protect and defend the people and property within their charge. This is the principle of legitimate authority. It makes an important distinction: it is the role of government, not private citizens, to provide this protection, whether it be law enforcement thwarting and arresting criminals or military operations to defeat terrorists or international criminal networks or to counter foreign attacks. Private citizens are generally not authorized to use lethal force, but President Roosevelt, as commander in chief, was the right person to oversee protection and defense—that is, the prosecution of the war. Congress complied with his request and declared war on December 8, 1941.

FDR's Address to Congress, December 8, 1941

Mr. Vice President, and Mr. Speaker, and Members of the Senate and House of Representatives:

Yesterday, December 7, 1941—a date which will live in infamy—the United States of America was suddenly and deliberately attacked by naval and air forces of the Empire of Japan.

The United States was at peace with that nation. . . .

It will be recorded that the distance of Hawaii from Japan makes it obvious that the attack was deliberately planned many days or even weeks ago. During the intervening time, the Japanese government has deliberately sought to deceive the United States by false statements and expressions of hope for continued peace. . . .

Japan has, therefore, undertaken a surprise offensive extending throughout the Pacific area [Hong Kong, Guam, Philippines, Wake, Midway]. . . .

As Commander in Chief of the Army and Navy, I have directed that all measures be taken for our defense.

But always will our whole nation remember the character of the onslaught against us.

No matter how long it may take us to overcome this premeditated invasion, the American people in their righteous might will win through to absolute victory. . . .

There is no blinking at the fact that our people, our territory, and our interests are in grave danger.

With confidence in our armed forces—with the unbounding determination of our people—we will gain the inevitable triumph—so help us God.

I ask that the Congress declare that since the unprovoked and dastardly attack by Japan on Sunday, December 7, 1941, a state of war has existed between the United States and the Japanese empire.

Source: Franklin Delano Roosevelt, "Joint Address to Congress Leading to a Declaration of War against Japan (1941)," National Archives, https://www.archives.gov/milestone-documents/joint-address-to-congress-declaration-of-war-against-japan.

"Protect and defend" suggests that there are just and unjust grounds for governments to employ military force. Just war statecraft asserts that just causes for using force are generally defensive in some way. In the fifth century, Augustine argued that just causes include protecting the vulnerable, punishing wrongdoers, and pre-venting additional wrong.[6] All three of these just causes are important roles for legitimate authority, and all three are limited. For instance, government must always be vigilant about protecting the vulnerable and preventing harm. A country is less likely to be attacked if it demonstrates a high level of security preparedness. In other words, deterrence (prevention) is a just cause for investing in a powerful and prepared military. At times, national defense requires a more active posture, as occurred in the US response to Pearl Harbor. The US responded by fighting back and ultimately defeating Japan.

"Punishment" as a just cause is highly contextual. At home, do-mestic law enforcement has courts, prisons, and a constitutional legal apparatus. The arena of war between nation-states is different. We will look at the concepts of retribution (punishment of aggression) and restoration (restitution for victims), both of which are politically and financially challenging during conflict and after war's end.

Legitimate authorities may employ military force on behalf of a *just cause*, but they are required to do so with proper ethical motiva-tions. This is what just war statecraft calls *right intention*. Augustine writes that greed, hatred, and lust are sinful motivations, but love of neighbor and the desire to thwart evil are appropriate motivations to use force in the pursuit of peace.[7]

At the time of the Pearl Harbor attack, Japan had a history of ag-gression, including three previous wars against either China or Russia in the previous forty years. In 1931, Japan launched its campaign to subdue or enslave large parts of Chinese territory, a campaign that developed over time into what may be best described as the "Three Alls Policy": "Burn all, kill all, loot all." On December 7, 1941, Japan launched coordinated attacks from Singapore to Hawaii. Tokyo's premeditated assaults on its neighbors were in no way a war with just cause and right intention. A response to this aggression from Washington and its allies, however, was clearly a just cause and could be motivated by right intention: to prevent additional harm by pun-ishing the attackers. Roosevelt spoke of bringing "righteous might" to bear against Japan with a determination to "triumph" and end such threats to the American people. Note that he did not speak of hating the Japanese people, nor did he use the language of bitter vengeance or dehumanize the enemy.

This is just war statecraft's foundation: legitimate political authorities have a responsibility to protect and defend those in their charge (just cause) and should do so with restraint in motivation and action (right intention). Just war statecraft also provides secondary, prudential criteria about how to make practical decisions in the context of national security threats. Among these are the *likelihood of success* and the *proportionality of ends.* Is a military response proportionate to the threat or grievance? In the case of Pearl Harbor and related attacks across the Pacific region, the answer was obviously affirmative.

Just war statesmen also must consider the likelihood of success of their strategies. We expect leaders to be good stewards of the resources at their disposal, from tax dollars to the lives of the men and women at their command. We expect leaders to carefully count the cost of various courses of action and direct their policies toward peace and security, not costly vengeance. The final condition of just war statecraft is reaching the conclusion that all other options have been exhausted and the restrained use of force is the only remaining possibility for restoring peace. This criterion is referred to as reasonable *last resort.* On December 7, 1941, the US and Japan were in the process of serious diplomatic negotiations. Previously, the US had imposed an oil embargo to criticize and restrict Japan's horrific attacks on civilians in China. After December 7, the use of force truly was a last resort for the US.

When the decision to go to war has been made, there are three just war criteria for how war is fought: *military necessity*, *proportionality*, and *discrimination* (i.e., making right distinctions). Each emphasizes stewardship and restraint. Military necessity is the basic concept that military leaders on the ground should make every effort at battlefield victory to achieve the just cause using lawful means. Necessity is balanced by proportionality, meaning that the weapons and tactics employed on a particular battlefield at a particular time should be proportionate to the type of fighting occurring. It would be ridiculous and disproportionate to obliterate a sniper with a squadron of bombers. Proportionality involves appropriate battlefield restraint, which makes war less destructive and less costly. Similarly, reasonable efforts should be made to distinguish between military targets and nonmilitary targets. This is the principle of discrimination. It is appropriate to attack the enemy's armed forces, military bases, and equipment. It is wrong to deliberately target civilians, private property, houses of worship, public buildings such as libraries and hospitals, and other such places. In international law this principle is called "noncombatant immunity."

When it came to the US response to the Japanese, or the British response to Nazi Germany, the campaigns were long, hard-fought, and expensive. The focus of battlefield military necessity was typically a blend of troop protection—considering how to best protect our troops from the enemy—with bold actions directed toward victory. One example of how the US and the British attempted to apply proportionality and discrimination occurred in the North African campaign, led by General Dwight D. Eisenhower. Not only did the Allies attempt to fight the Nazi Panzer divisions away from cities and villages, but Eisenhower issued booklets to the troops on how to treat the local Arab Muslims respectfully.

Just war statecraft's goal is *peace*. At war's end, governments should look to establish three conditions for an enduring and secure peace. Those three conditions, or principles, are *order*, *justice*, and *conciliation*. Order means that the basic functions of governance and security are being administered within the former war zones. Postconflict restoration of justice may include steps to hold aggressors accountable and provide some sort of restoration to survivors and victims. Although it is difficult to achieve, over time some form of conciliation may be possible. Conciliation means coming to terms with the past in such a way that one can imagine a different future— one where former adversaries are no longer the enemy.

World War II began grotesquely, with bombs falling on London and later on Pearl Harbor. The war crimes and devastation were truly appalling. Due to the radical evil of the Nazi and Japanese systems, Roosevelt and Churchill determined that the Axis powers must unconditionally surrender. When they did so, the Allies moved in and immediately began to provide order. Unlike the Soviet occupation of Eastern Europe, which was vindictive and violent, the Western Allies' postwar activities in ravaged Japan and Germany established a just order in those countries. Western armies provided security, food, and essential goods to help them. Over the next few years, the Marshall Plan helped rebuild Western Europe and Japan, whereas the Soviets refused aid to countries they occupied.

The victorious Western allies imposed the Nuremberg and Tokyo war crimes tribunals on both countries, but it was just a few dozen senior leaders who faced retribution. Over time, the German government indicted another two thousand individuals—a tiny number compared to all involved in the murderous Nazi regime. These steps at bringing aggressors to justice, though, were extremely important in moving these societies beyond the legacy of the past and toward a better future. Under Western protection and guidance, West Germany and Japan became integrated into Western institutions such as the United Nations, NATO and its Asian counterpart (SEATO), and the early European Union. Gradually, a limited amount of conciliation grew between the former adversaries. Just war statecraft is focused from beginning to end on the goal of peace. As President Roosevelt stated in an earlier address,

> If civilization is to survive, the principles of the Prince of Peace must be restored. Shattered trust between nations must be revived.
>
> Most important of all, the will for peace on the part of peace-loving nations must express itself to the end that nations that may be tempted to violate their agreements and the rights of others will desist from such a cause. There must be positive endeavors to preserve peace.
>
> America hates war. America hopes for peace. Therefore, America actively engages in the search for peace.[8]

Principles of Just War Statecraft

Jus ad Bellum (The Morality of Going to War)

- *Legitimate authority*: Legitimate political authorities in a jurisdiction are morally responsible for the security of their constituents and therefore are obligated to make decisions about war and peace.

- *Just cause*: Self-defense of citizens' lives, livelihoods, and way of life are typically just causes; more generally speaking, the cause is likely just if it rights a past wrong, punishes wrongdoers, or prevents further wrong.

- *Right intention*: Political motivations are subject to ethical scrutiny; force intended for the purpose of order, justice, and ultimate conciliation is just, whereas violence for the sake of hatred, revenge, and destruction is not just.

- *Likelihood of success*: Political leaders should consider whether their action will make a difference in real-world outcomes. This principle is subject to context and judgment, because it may be appropriate to act despite a low likelihood of success (e.g., against local genocide). Conversely, it may be inappropriate to act due to low efficacy despite the compelling nature of the case.

- *Proportionality of ends*: Does the preferred outcome justify, in terms of the cost in lives and material resources, this course of action?

- *Last resort*: Have traditional diplomatic and other efforts been reasonably employed in order to avoid outright bloodshed?

Jus in Bello (The Morality of Fighting War)

- *Military necessity*: Is every reasonable effort made to gain battlefield advantage in pursuit of larger strategic objectives in the cause of justice, while restrained by law and other *jus in bello* criteria?

- *Proportionality*: Are the battlefield tools and tactics employed proportionate to battlefield objectives?

- *Discrimination*: Have distinctions been drawn to reasonably protect the lives and property of noncombatants?

Jus post Bellum (The Morality of How War Ends)

- *Order*: Legitimate authority has the capacity to provide basic government services and security from internal or external threats.
- *Justice*: Establishing a just peace may include consideration of individual punishment for those who violated the law of armed conflict and restitution policies for victims when appropriate.
- *Conciliation*: The parties should come to terms with the past so that they can imagine and move forward toward a shared future.

Looking Ahead

Thus far I have introduced just war statecraft as a responsible, principled course of action to seek peace. Chapter 2, "Theological Foundations of Just War Statecraft," goes into some detail on the theological underpinnings of the just war principles of legitimate political authority acting on a just cause with right intentions. The Bible teaches, from the Old Testament through Romans 13 and other passages, that God instituted a basic principle of *governance* in human affairs and created a set of natural authority structures—often called "institutions"—including the family and government (political authority). Protestants call this diversity of sectors and institutions, which includes the important role of a strong but limited political authority, *sphere sovereignty* (Roman Catholics have a slightly different view called *subsidiarity*).

Chapter 2 also looks at the Protestant doctrine of *calling* or *vocation*. God gives everyone skills and talents that provide value to the community. God calls people into many forms of service, whether in the church or outside it. These professions are part of the warp and woof of society, and therefore, the call to public service, including military service, is a call to a noble profession.

Augustine, Aquinas, Luther, Calvin, Wesley, and many others agreed that just causes for using force include protecting the weak, punishing the wrongdoer, righting past wrongs, and preventing future wrong. In other words, they concur that *justice is the cause for which legitimate authorities may use force.* They also argued, based on biblical teaching, that *motivations* matter. God told Samuel that he looked on the heart, not the outward appearance (1 Sam. 16:7). Jesus taught that it is intentions and desire that are the focal point for sin (Matt. 5). What should be our motivating ethic, whether in personal relationships or in our callings? Love of God and love of neighbor (Greek: *agapē*; Latin: *caritas*, or charity [1 Cor. 13]). Augustine's letters to soldiers as well as his *City of God* suggest that those who protect and defend should be acting on God-inspired love of neighbor, love of community, and love of country. This also limits appropriate patriotism from becoming any form of political idolatry or collective chauvinism, such as ethnic nationalism or totalitarian socialism.

Chapter 2 emphasizes the biblical principle of *stewardship*. Leaders should count the cost before going to war. Just war thinking has long included prudential considerations about the use of diplomacy before force, including the criteria of likelihood of success and last resort. Similarly, when force is employed, one must use only the amount of force that is proportionate to battlefield objectives and take care in distinguishing between legitimate and illegitimate targets in order to protect civilian life and property (using the just war criterion of discrimination). Recent international law has distilled these principles as prohibitions to limit suffering, adopting a principle that has clearly been a value of Christians for millennia.

"Historical Overview of the Christian Just War Tradition" (chap. 3) is a historical survey of the Christian just war tradition and the enduring issue motivating theologians, philosophers, and statesmen: *How do we establish and maintain peace?* This chapter begins with a careful defining of key concepts, distinguishing, for instance, between a morally healthy peace and an "iniquitous peace." The latter is the sort of immoral order imposed by victorious Nazis or Communists. We will look at some of the key Christian contributors who helped refine thinking on peace among governments and nations, including Augustine, Aquinas, Luther, and Calvin and, more recently,

Paul Ramsey, Jean Bethke Elshtain, and others. For instance, in the sixteenth century a Roman Catholic priest named Francisco de Vitoria advanced the concept of "noncombatant immunity" (protecting enemy civilians) based on their moral worth as God's creation. In our own time, evangelical scholar J. Daryl Charles has written extensively on the moral imperative to stop ethnic cleansing and genocide. A recurring theme of chapter 3 is Christian just war thinkers applying these ethical principles to the moral dilemmas of their time, working out appropriate limits on warriors and warfighting, all with the goal of peace.

The previous chapters laid out the principles that underlie just war statecraft and their rootedness in key biblical doctrines such as neighbor-love, stewardship, and vocation. It is fairly easy for most of us to see the application of those principles in most cases, such as intervening to stop the genocide of innocent Iraqis and Syrians at the hands of ISIS or acting out of self-defense and pursuing justice after Pearl Harbor or 9/11. But there remain a number of recurring "what if" questions when it comes to justice and violence. They typically revolve around two large issues for Christians. The first has to do with a range of activities that appear to be rebellion against political authority: civil disobedience, terrorism, armed resistance, and revolution.

Chapter 4, "Morality and Contemporary Warfare," deals with many of these issues by distinguishing the elements of lawful resistance from unlawful violence and rebellion. The key is to make appropriate distinctions. When citizens or groups resist, their intentions and their behavior tell us a great deal about their desired objectives. Our framework for investigating these categories is based on making right distinctions, such as between legitimate and illegitimate authority, between right and wrong intentions, and especially between force and violence. I will apply these distinctions to historical cases such as the American War for Independence, resistance to Hitler's Germany, and the US civil rights movement.

Chapter 4 also considers a second issue that raises many questions, the seemingly unrestrained warfare of the books of Judges and Joshua and, by extension, the Crusades of the eleventh through thirteenth centuries. Is the Old Testament account synonymous with the Crusades? What about forms of so-called holy war, such as violent Islamist terrorism? We will carefully look at authority, intentions, and actions as we consider these important issues. One general comment can be made now: those who say the ends justify the means, *any means*, as terrorists like Osama bin Laden and Che Guevara did, are operating from principles antithetical to a Christian worldview. Christians know that *how one fights* is just as important as *what one fights for*.

Chapter 5, "The Motivations and Characteristics of Just Warriors," considers the moral preparation and character of our guardians and protectors. Not every soldier or sailor will become a hero like America's legendary Sergeant York, but we want every member of our armed forces to develop the virtues that are displayed by the hero in moments of crisis. This chapter explores our society's framing of heroes, from battlefield veterans to fictional characters such as Harry Potter and Luke Skywalker. Just warriors are distinguished by *what they love*, *what angers them*, and their *character*. We will explore rightful love of country (patriotism) and love of comrades. We will also look at the important distinction between righteous indignation in response to injustice, on the one hand, and wrongful hatred, on the other. Just like Jesus in the temple, the just warrior may become angry but should never give in to vengeful wrath. The four *cardinal virtues*—prudence, justice, temperance, and fortitude— provide a foundation for the heart of the just warrior.

Chapter 6, "Ending Wars Well," brings us full circle to considering peace at conflict's end. The chapter starts with a three-part framework: order, justice, and conciliation. A secure and enduring peace must start with basic governance and security (order) and establish elements of justice (punishment of wrong, restitution to victims). Christians, motivated by love and hope, should constantly be looking for prudential ways to do what Lewis suggested at Oxford: "To avert or postpone one particular war by wise policy, or to render one particular campaign shorter by strength and skill or less terrible by mercy to the conquered and the civilians is more useful than all the proposals for universal peace that have ever been made."[9] Moreover, efforts to secure the peace and advance justice lay the foundations for conciliation and political forgiveness. We have seen this in the years following World War II, at Camp David's treaty between Israel and Egypt in 1979, after the Rwandan genocide, and elsewhere. In these contexts, idealistic notions of simply "forgiving and forgetting" too often prove merely aspirational and unrealistic, because they fail to undertake the extraordinarily hard work of political conciliation. This chapter provides a number of modern examples of biblically inspired postconflict conciliation, including President Lincoln's desire for national reconciliation rather than vengeance, Archbishop Desmond Tutu's influence on South Africa's postapartheid Truth and Reconciliation Commission, and Christian peacemakers in Mozambique.

Chapter 6 also argues that some Christians have vocational roles to play across the entire spectrum of domestic and international conflict. Some are called to be just warriors. Others are called to work to prevent war, assuage the grief of victims, rebuild societies through humanitarian aid, or work in the justice sector. Christian thinking on national security stewardship suggests that we need Christians in all walks of life who can serve the common good in their vocations, including when the bullets are flying and thereafter. Our pastors need to preach this. Our parishioners need to pray for the wisdom of leaders, for peace in our society and beyond, and for the success of public servants in their work on behalf of the common good. Exploring these dimensions is the purpose of this book.

2

Theological Foundations
of Just War Statecraft

Governance, Calling, and Stewardship

With the threat of attack looming, Nehemiah armed the men working on Jerusalem's defenses, instituting a watch system with half the men standing guard at any given time. As governor of Judea, Nehemiah dealt not only with budgets and bureaucracies but with ongoing resistance from those who should have been his allies. He even faced a potential conspiracy to assassinate him. His enemies undermined his authority by accusing him of treason to his boss, the king of Persia. In short, Nehemiah faced a lack of security, violence, and looming disaster.

The story of Nehemiah provides a useful example for thinking about the biblical foundations of just war statecraft. This chapter is divided into two parts. The first part examines three biblical doctrines that provide a foundation for thinking about statecraft and the principles of governance, vocation, and stewardship. The second part of the chapter builds on this foundation by laying out some of the key principles of Christian just war statecraft. The just war tradition argues that legitimate authorities may threaten or use force on behalf of just causes when acting on right intentions. As stewards of public resources, government officials should count the cost in a number of ways, such as considering the likelihood of success of various courses of action. The story of Nehemiah brings many of these elements together, reminding us that before we think about how war is fought, we must begin with the responsibilities of those entrusted with securing the peace.

Order, Institutions, and Government

Nehemiah was an exile from Judah, one of the tens of thousands deported to Babylon. God had promised restoration to Judah, but in the meantime the exiled Jews were enjoined to flourish where they were. Many did. We know the stories of important public officials including Daniel, Shadrach, Meshach, Abednego, Mordecai, and Esther—Jews who rose to the pinnacle of responsibility and influence in a foreign land. The book of Nehemiah is set in this context of an imperial capital, with Nehemiah at the center of power. Like Daniel or Mordecai, Nehemiah holds a position of ultimate trust: he is cupbearer to the king. This means that he is on hand to sample the king's beverages lest they be poisoned. It is likely that Nehemiah would have had similar training to that of Daniel and his friends: "people of Israel, both of the royal family and of the nobility, youths without blemish, of good appearance and skillful in all wisdom, endowed with knowledge, understanding learning, and competent to stand in the king's palace" (Dan. 1:3–4).

Nehemiah was part of an elite civil service and would have mastered court etiquette, spoken multiple languages, and cultivated a variety of skills and talents. Beyond his formal education, Nehemiah gained experience through service, ultimately rising to this trusted position as cupbearer. Day after day and night after night Nehemiah was on hand to hear the king and his senior counselors discuss matters of state. There could scarcely have been better leadership preparation than this, especially for the grandchild of conquered Jews.

Nehemiah's tale is one of daring, intrigue, danger, and prayerful action: this is statecraft in action. He served as a Persian governor of Judea for twelve years, rebuilt the walls of Jerusalem, faced death threats, and inspired the downtrodden Jews to realize God's purpose for their time. He dealt with strategic planning, finance, fickle public opinion, uncertain friends, and personal exhaustion just like any great servant leader. Nehemiah did not seek out enemies, but he zealously sought to deter their influence on the spiritual and material rebuilding of Jerusalem. Nehemiah exemplifies public servants whose love of neighbor, love of country, and love of God motivate them to outstanding service.

In Nehemiah's story, we take much for granted. For instance, we accept that political order is naturally necessary for human flourishing. We recognize lawlessness and disorder as threats. That is because God has ordained that humans live in social relationships and, to superintend this, has ordained a basic principle of governance or order. Typically, the way that we govern and are governed is through institutions. When one hears the word "institution," one usually thinks of an imposing building like those that house the Supreme Court of the United States or the United Nations. But, at its heart, an institution is about relationships, particularly the rules and expectations, formal and informal, that govern those relationships. The family is, therefore, an institution. There are many other institutions, from the local PTA to complex organizations like NATO and the United States Department of Justice.

The Bible gives us at least three institutions and suggests that human creativity may organize others. Each is the appropriate *authority* for establishing and maintaining *order* (governance) within its sphere. Those three primary institutions are the family, the church, and government. God established the family in Genesis as the principal social unit: "It is not good that the man should be alone" (Gen.

2:18). Jesus affirms, "Therefore a man shall leave his father and his mother and hold fast to his wife, and the two shall become one flesh" (Matt. 19:5). The family is the first institution of society, with its own authority structure (parents). The family is the institution where children are raised, obligations are shared between old and young, and values are transmitted across the generations.

A second institution is the church, in which Christians as the body of believers assemble for corporate worship and discipleship (Heb. 10:25). The church is also to be a center for evangelism and charity. The church as an institution has a governance model: structured leadership (pastors, elders, deacons), rules for sustainability (e.g., tithes and offerings), and principles for resolving internal disputes and even excommunicating those who violate the basic strictures of the community.[1]

A third institution is political authority or government. Romans 13 tells us that rulers are instituted for the common good. However, the Bible does not set up a single model for how people must organize themselves (e.g., as a monarchy or democracy). The Bible has a lot to say to leaders about acting as good stewards of finite resources and about promoting security and justice (e.g., Prov. 24:6; Luke 14:28). The Old Testament provides a general set of principles about citizenship, law, and justice and is replete with examples of political and military leaders, such as Joseph, Moses, Joshua, David, Hezekiah, Nehemiah, and Daniel. Paul and Peter admonish citizens to honor and pray for their leaders (e.g., 1 Tim. 2:1–2; 1 Pet. 2:17).

The family, the church, and political authority are not the only institutions in human society. The Bible also assumes many other sectors of human gifting and activity: agriculture, commerce, literature, science, music, and the like. In practice, people tend to organize themselves, cooperating in man-made institutions with their own rules and internal authority structures. Indeed, it is a mark of God's imprint on humanity for people to organize, establish new institutions, and cooperate to solve problems, whether the new institution be a labor union, a business enterprise, a symphony orchestra, or a school. Humans are naturally social, and institutions are often the outcome of our cooperative efforts to pursue goals together.

Reflecting on these created realities, Christians have developed ways of describing the relationships of institutions and various sectors of public life. Roman Catholics have developed a principle called "subsidiarity," which states that a problem or issue should be dealt with by the institution closest to it. At the individual level, families are the first defense against poverty and need. If the family breaks down in some way, or it is not suited to meet the threat, then it should look outside of itself for help at the local level (neighborhood, local church, etc.). Most needs can be met at this level by extended family and friends, the trading of goods and services in the marketplace (e.g., grocery store, medical services, local government), the local church, and local charities.

If the family and local assistance are not adequate, then the need may have to be met at the next level of society. In the US, with our federal system of government, we see this as the distribution of responsibility between local, state, and national governments. Some responsibilities are most fitting for one level, such as child-rearing for the family and national defense for the federal government in Washington, DC. Subsidiarity, then, is one way of describing the dynamics of a healthy society, demonstrating that some responsibilities—such as law enforcement, the judiciary, and the military—are reserved for specific government authorities.

A complementary idea has developed in the Protestant tradition. This is the framework known as "sphere sovereignty," expressed by Dutch theologian, journalist, and prime minister Abraham Kuyper (1837–1920). Sphere sovereignty is the idea that many sectors of social life (e.g., business, education, government, agriculture, science) are important avenues for human flourishing. All of these sectors, and the institutions they represent, are accountable to God, who gave humanity the skills and talents useful for human flourishing. Kuyper described a cohesive society as one that functions like a sophisticated timepiece. Imagine all of the independent gears that interlock and work collectively to make Big Ben function. Each gear represents a sector of society (economics, politics, religion, the arts, agriculture, media, sport, etc.). Each gear, or sector, of society has competencies and authority within its own sphere of influence, but they operate cooperatively for the good of society as a whole.

Sphere sovereignty reminds us that most of life lived together in society is not the partisan screaming we hear on the nightly news. Washington, DC, is not the center of the universe. Rather, the vast majority of social life for most people in most places takes place in other sectors and institutions than political government. Each of these institutions, from a soccer league to a religious denomination, expresses internal governance (order and authority) in its own way via charters, bylaws, election of officers, and the like. Sphere sovereignty is tied to the doctrine of vocation, as it reminds us that just as some have a vocational expertise in business, farming, or science, some are called to the vocation of public service: elected office, law enforcement, the courts, the armed forces. Every sector is needed for society to function properly.

In sum, God initiated institutions such as the family and government while also giving humanity tremendous latitude about how to steward the world that he gave to us. Christians should not fall into the trap of thinking that everything must be "political." God ordained an important role for government, but it is just one type of institution among many others. Christians need to think more broadly about the well-being of society, especially the healthy independence of sectors such as business, education, religious institutions, the medical sector, and so on, as well as these sectors' interdependence for human flourishing. This view properly limits the power of government to its own sphere of influence, and one can see how America's constitutional principles of checks and balances, separation of powers, and federalism (division of power between federal, state, and local governments) are one way, though not the only way, of putting sphere sovereignty and subsidiarity into practice. This underscores the importance of just war statecraft: we need law enforcement and the military to protect the peaceful occupations of all society's institutions.

Vocation and Calling

At various times throughout history, Christians have allowed a divide between the "sacred" and "secular" to spread into their view of service. When this happens, callings that have to do with the church and Christian ministry are seen as service to God while other jobs are viewed as second-class, simply paying the bills, the necessary toil of life on earth. Those jobs are not spiritually significant. This view is wrong.

Instead, the Bible teaches that God has superintended much of the world through human agency. He has given humanity a vast multitude of skills, talents, and abilities to be used for the common good. God has given gifts to every person, and he calls each person to use the entirety of their life to glorify him and serve others. All of the callings are useful and good.[2]

In the Bible Bezalel and Oholiab (Exod. 31:1–11) were skilled craftsmen who built the tabernacle and the various implements needed when Israel left Egypt. Jubal (Gen. 4:21), Asaph (1 Chron. 6:31–48; Pss. 73–83), and others were skilled musicians and lyricists. Moses set up an administrative court system composed of wise leaders (Exod. 18). David and his generals set up a military structure of command and administration that defeated Israel's enemies, culminating in Solomon's levies and massive building programs (1 Chron. 22; 28). The New Testament records centurions, those working in Caesar's household, merchants, and even a lawyer named Zenas as members of the early church. Proverbs extols the skilled professions including the architect and the builder, the wise farmer, the political leader, and more.

So, the individual has God-given skills and talents that bring purpose to one's life, serve the body of Christ and society more generally, and, thus, promote the common good. All of us are called to do our work with technical proficiency: "Whatever you do, work heartily, as for the Lord and not for men" (Col. 3:23). We are also commanded to act with honesty and integrity, regardless of what that work is, treating others as we would like to be treated (Matt. 7:12). Society needs pastors, doctors, teachers, and lawyers in order to be healthy. We also need warriors and guardians to protect and defend. In sum, those called to be judges, police officers, politicians, and military personnel are to serve their fellow citizens by promoting law and order, punishing wrongdoers, righting past wrongs, seeking the common good, establishing and preserving security, and protecting the vulnerable. Just war statecraft affirms that God calls some people to the vocation of protecting and defending, just as he did Nehemiah, Joseph, and David, and therefore Christians in these professions should be both technical experts and Christian salt and light.

Stewardship

The idea of authority and stewardship arises early in the Bible, in Genesis 1:26–28:

> Then God said, "Let us make man in our image, after our likeness. And let them have dominion over the fish of the sea and over the birds of the heavens and over the livestock and over all the earth and over every creeping thing that creeps on the earth." So God created man in his own image, in the image of God he created him; male and female he created them. And God blessed them. And God said to them, "Be fruitful and multiply and fill the earth and subdue it, and have dominion over the fish of the sea and over the birds of the heavens and over every living thing that moves on the earth."

The words "dominion" and "subdue" elsewhere often describe the wrongful use of power. But here the Bible is teaching an energetic form of stewardship in which humanity is charged with managing the earth and its resources in a way that is accountable to God as Lord over all. This is the principle of stewardship. In this context the term "dominion" should be thought of not as domination, but as connoting a domain of responsibility. God assigns humanity a domain in which to live in a way that glorifies him by caring for his creation. That domain—our area of responsibility—is the earth.

One author defines "stewardship" as "utilizing and managing all resources God provides for the glory of God and the betterment of His creation."[3] Another says, "An essential aspect of biblical stewardship is looking after people and providing order over Creation."[4] In short, people are entrusted with stewardship: managing, caretaking, superintending, and overseeing God's creation in the domains that they are called to (vocation). Interestingly, in Greek the term "steward" (*oikonomos*) is closely related to the word "economy" (*oikonomia*). Stewards economize. It is no surprise, therefore, that Jesus would say, "Which of you, desiring to build a tower, does not first sit down and count the cost?" (Luke 14:28), or that Jesus would describe effective stewardship in the parable of the talents (Matt. 25:14–30). Those domains, or spheres of responsibility, range from the family to the church, schools and universities, agriculture, science, business, and other sectors. One of those domains is the wide arena of government and national security affairs.

Stewardship is a coin with two sides: *responsibility* and *accountability*. God entrusted the management of creation in all its aspects to humankind. We are responsible to manage and care for whatever domain God has entrusted to our care. For public officials, this means the responsibility to protect and defend the citizenry from criminality and violence. Citizens should hold leaders accountable for providing order, security, and justice. Our society is made up of networks of responsibility and accountability, from families to the federal government. The entry-level worker is accountable to his boss; the boss is responsible to pay and empower the worker. Even the president of the United States is accountable to tax-paying citizens.

In sum, God affirms the principle of order in Genesis 1:28, Romans 13, and elsewhere. Whether it is an Old Testament patriarch, a judge, a monarch, or a military officer, they are agents equipped to promote order and the common good. They should see their roles as stewards of God's world order and of his people. Leaders are expected to count the cost of their policies through sound economic judgment and the counsel of others. Public officials have a responsibility to God and their fellow citizens to act for the best interests of the community and are accountable for their actions.

Just War Principles Rooted in Governance, Calling, and Stewardship

Thus far in this chapter we have looked at the foundational principles of governance, vocation, and stewardship. All of these principles can be found in Nehemiah's story. As governor, Nehemiah was responsible for the security of the people under his charge. We can see that he did not aggressively seek controversy or conflict, but he stood his ground courageously when faced with threats and opposition. He could do so, in part, because his cause was just and his intentions were morally sound.

This brings us to the primary formal criteria of just war statecraft. Scholars call the first three just war principles "deontological," meaning they have to do with the moral obligations leaders have when considering the use of force. The first principle is legitimate authority. Legitimate political authorities are morally responsible for the security of their constituents and therefore are obligated to make decisions about war and peace. Nehemiah was delegated that responsibility by the king of Persia. Nehemiah, therefore, had to make decisions about how best to defend the people under his charge and fulfill the mission entrusted to him by the king. Nehemiah did this by careful planning, by a strategy of vigilance and armed deterrence, and by avoiding traps, such as a ruse to assassinate him outside the city walls.

The second principle is just cause. Self-defense of citizens' lives, livelihoods, and way of life is typically a just cause. Moreover, the cause is likely just if it rights a past wrong, punishes wrongdoers, or prevents further wrong.[5] We need government—the legitimate authority—to be the focal point for decisions about just cause. Thankfully, there are people like Nehemiah, who are called to a variety of public service vocations to assess threats and then act to promote peace and security. It is noteworthy that Nehemiah focuses his attention on specific threats, such as Sanballat and his henchmen, rather than on amorphous enemies and conspiracy theories. Nehemiah was not looking for a fight, but he was justified in defending Jerusalem.

The third principle of the historic just war criteria is right intention. Leaders are morally accountable for their motivations: they do not get a pass because they are in a position of authority. Political motivations are subject to ethical scrutiny; force intended for the purpose of order, justice, and ultimate conciliation is just, whereas violence, for the sake of hatred, revenge, and destruction, is not just. Right intention is emphasized throughout the Bible. God explained to Samuel that he looks on the heart, rather than on outward appearances. Jesus warned of the internal sins of lust and hatred. We see the difference that motives make in the decades-long relationship of King David and his general Joab. Both David and Joab could be ruthless, but David's penitent and conciliatory spirit made him a man after God's own heart, whereas Joab appears to have been a man of expediency and vengeance.

No leader, from Moses to Winston Churchill, has had infinite wisdom and infinite resources at his or her disposal. Political leaders do not simply operate on the plane of abstract morality but must also consider the tangible factors of every situation. This is the Christian principle of stewardship, and it is of great importance for just war statecraft. However, the question is, How do a country's leaders put stewardship into action, particularly when it comes to diplomacy and the use of force? Just war thinkers have developed a number of criteria for national security stewardship that are rooted in the responsibility that leaders have for careful management of resources and obligations. Some of these principles have to do with how leaders "count the cost" when making the decision to prepare for, or engage in, armed conflict (scholars call this *jus ad bellum*, or the morality of going to war). Other just war principles have to do with how war is fought (*jus in bello*, the morality of fighting war) and the ethics of peacefully ending war (*jus post bellum*).

I have already said that political authorities should orient themselves morally on just cause and right intention. The decision may be to prepare or act in some way, but the decision may also be not to act. These decisions are informed by the prudential stewardship criteria of likelihood of success, proportionality of ends, and last resort.

As mentioned earlier, prudence dictates that political leaders consider whether any action will make a difference in real-world outcomes. This principle of likelihood of success is subject to context and judgment, including careful consideration of the multi-dimensionality of "success." At the time of this writing, the 2022 Russian invasion of Ukraine has riveted world attention for months. If Ukraine had followed the conventional wisdom and surrendered a large part of its territory at the moment of invasion, on the notion that Ukraine could not succeed against Russia, we would never have seen the valiant and efficacious defense of Ukraine that will undoubtedly save much of its territory. Moreover, that defense allowed millions of civilians to flee the Russian onslaught and provided vital time for Western leaders to decide to provide armaments. Thoughtful leaders think carefully about what success means, such as keeping open vital humanitarian corridors to rescue noncombatants, even at a high price to soldiers, or holding out long enough for allies to prepare and join the fight. A principle such as likelihood of success reminds us how valuable extensive preparation and training of leaders is so that they can make wise decisions.

A second stewardship principle that is important for judging the right response based on national security grievances is proportionality of ends. Does the preferred outcome justify, in terms of the cost in lives and material resources, this course of action? Presidents and prime ministers often publicly assert their "war aims." The nature of democracy is such that many of today's leaders must publicly explain their rationale for going to war and their vision for a better state of peace at war's end.

A final stewardship principle for the decision to go to war is last resort. Have traditional diplomatic and other efforts been reasonably employed in order to avoid outright bloodshed? This principle reminds us that the decision to authorize military force is not made in a vacuum. National security officials consider the full range of tools at their disposal. Soldiers and diplomats use the acronym DIME for these "four elements of national power," which include diplomacy, information and intelligence, military power, and economic statecraft.[6] The decisions of when to defend an ally, intervene against genocide, or protect one's own citizens, and the best strategic means of doing so, are constantly being analyzed and debated by national security experts. Last resort does not mean waiting too long, to the point of extinction or slavery. It means counting the cost, taking deliberative steps that include warnings and deterrence, and involving all aspects of national power, from public cautions to private diplomacy to sanctions to espionage, as part of the ongoing effort to protect one's country and reinforce global security.

Before looking at the stewardship principles of how war is fought, consider how the six just war principles we have looked at thus far are similar to the way that a surgeon makes a decision about amputating a limb. Qualified surgeons (authority) are highly competent. Their purpose is to preserve and save human life (just cause). We want surgeons to be motivated primarily by what is best for the patient, not wealth or status (right intention). Indeed, a focus on wealth or status might make a surgeon either too risk-averse ("Despite my world-class skills, I don't want to harm my reputation for 100 percent perfect results") or too risk-seeking ("I'll always 'go for it,' regardless of survivability or the patient's wishes"). The surgeon makes decisions that are commensurate with the stewardship principles we have outlined. To be sure, amputating an arm or a leg is "force." However, this is no time to be a surgical "pacifist" and avoid causing pain. Amputation is, in a sense, a last resort action that is undertaken when a careful consideration of all the restorative options (likelihood of success) have been considered toward the goal of saving a life (proportionality of ends). Amputating a limb may be a "good" in protecting an injured soldier from gangrene and death. Amputation allows the soldier to return home to their family rather than die on the battlefield. We need skilled medical practitioners who are strategic in making such decisions, just as we need morally rooted, skillful national security leaders.

A second arena of stewardship has to do with how force is employed after political authorities have decided to do so. These three principles apply to law enforcement as well as to the armed forces. The first is necessity or military necessity, which is the idea that every reasonable and lawful effort should be made to gain battlefield advantage—to win in a particular place and time—in pursuit of larger strategic objectives that advance a just cause. "Lawful effort" means that the tools and decisions of warfare must conform to, and be restrained by, the law of armed conflict. The US has been a leader in writing and advancing the law of armed conflict for more than 150 years. For instance, in 1863, President Lincoln instituted new rules regulating military conduct that are widely known as the Lieber Code, so named after Professor Francis Lieber. That code, based in classic just war reasoning, spread throughout Europe in the late nineteenth century and is the foundation for today's US Code of Military Justice (governing American military personnel) and a number of international covenants such as the Hague and Geneva Conventions that limit weapons such as poison gas and protect noncombatants. Almost all countries have formally agreed to observe these limitations.

The other stewardship principles for tactical, local decisions in battle are proportionality and discrimination. The former requires that battlefield tools and tactics be proportionate to battlefield objectives. It would be ridiculously disproportionate, and costly, to launch a nuclear missile to knock out a patrol boat. The weapons and tactics of warfare should be contextualized to achieving a restrained victory in this time and place by bringing to bear enough force to win without disproportionate damage. A good battlefield commander cares deeply about the lives of his own soldiers, the limited materiel available (e.g., ammunition, vehicles, rations), and decisively winning the engagement without catastrophic damage to the region. Proportionality works in collaboration with the principle of discrimination, or distinction, which is codified in international law as "noncombatant immunity." Commanders must consider how to reasonably protect the lives and property of legitimate noncombatants (e.g., civilians). In practice, this means protecting the many goods necessary for society to function, such as the electrical grid, water and sewage, houses of worship, schools, hospitals, and the like. In this regard, coalition forces in Iraq and Afghanistan in recent years exercised enormous constraint that caused great risk to US, Dutch, Canadian, British, Australian, and other forces. This was done in keeping with the principles of proportionality and discrimination. From smart bombs to restrictive rules of engagement to satellite imagery, much has been done to realize the full potential of these stewardship principles.

Conclusion: Nehemiah as a Just Statesman

When Nehemiah was authorized by the Persian king to serve as governor of Judea and rebuild the walls of Jerusalem, he behaved as we expect any great leader to do. He communicated, built a team, created a budget, developed a threat assessment, established a strategic plan, executed the work, maintained security vigilance, and completed the mission. He did all of this in conditions of great insecurity. Nehemiah not only worked hard but also relied on God. His urgent, passionate prayers for direction and assistance are an inspiration: "For they all wanted to frighten us, thinking, 'Their hands will drop from the work, and it will not be done.' But now, O God, strengthen my hands" (Neh. 6:9). Nehemiah reflects all the theological foundations of just war statecraft—legitimate government authority, a calling to public service, and stewardship. He also exemplifies the basic just war criteria of sophisticated planning and execution by legitimate political authorities acting on just causes with right intention. All of Nehemiah's work had a goal in mind, which was the peace and security of his fellow Jews living at home in Jerusalem and Judea. It is to that goal, the quest for peace, that we now turn.

3

Historical Overview of the Christian Just War Tradition

Pursuing Peace and the Problem with Pacifism

One of the most popular novels and film series of recent years is Suzanne Collins's *The Hunger Games*. Set in a future dystopian America that has survived an atomic civil war, the narrative portrays the country as having twelve provinces ruled by an arrogant and brutal elite. The capital, Panem ("bread" in Latin), is modeled on ancient Rome. It is a luxurious city supported, unequally and unwillingly, by the bonded labor of subjects in the provinces who provide the best food, fuel, and other resources to maintain the luxurious lifestyle of the citizens of Panem. At the heart of this degrading system is a gladiatorial contest, pitting adolescent fighters from each of the twelve districts against each other in a televised death match. The Hunger Games are a futuristic version of Rome's "bread and circuses," a sort of Super Bowl to the death.

The fighters are drawn by lot from each district's teenagers: one boy, one girl. What grips readers and cinema audiences is the gritty,

sacrificial role of the central heroine, Katniss Everdeen. Katniss stuns
the world of Panem by volunteering to fight in the Hunger Games in
the place of her twelve-year-old sister, whose name had been drawn
to appear in the contest. It is a moment of heroism, not because
of any accomplishment, but because of Katniss's sacrificial choice
to interpose herself and save her sister. It is an example of Christ's
teaching that there is no greater love than to lay down one's life for
another.

An entirely different perspective is provided by Panem's long-
serving President Coriolanus Snow. A prequel (*The Ballad of Song-
birds and Snakes*) tells us how the seventeen-year-old Snow barely
survived the hunger and destruction of the country's civil war. Sixty
years later, during the *Hunger Games* trilogy, President Snow is the
supreme advocate of a certain type of peace: a brutal victor's peace.
Over the decades Snow becomes a ruthless strategist who keeps the
capital's denizens content and dominates the provincials. His quasi-
mystical perspective on this peace is expressed early in the book:

> [Panem] rose up out of the ashes of a place that was once called North
> America. North America was destroyed with droughts, storms, fires,
> and other natural disasters. Then a brutal war took place over the
> land that remained. The result was Panem, a shining Capitol ringed
> by thirteen districts, which brought peace and prosperity to its citizens.
> Then came the Dark Days, the uprising of the districts against the
> Capitol. Twelve were defeated, the thirteenth obliterated. The Treaty
> of Treason gave us the new laws to guarantee peace and, as our yearly
> reminder that the Dark Days must never be repeated, it gave us the
> Hunger Games.[1]

Panem's peace is the pacification of any enemy, a rigid, unjust order
that benefits a small elite at the expense of the majority. Augustine
distinguishes between the "peace of the just" and the "peace of the
iniquitous." When the Soviets took over Russia, they enforced an
iniquitous peace at home and sought to impose it abroad. Hitler and
his Nazi regime sought a form of "peace" based on Aryan supremacy

and the enslavement of those they deemed inferior races and individuals. Panem's peace, too, is an iniquitous peace.

These examples show why it is critical to get our definitions of peace right. We cannot merely say that peace is the opposite of war. Just war statecraft understands peace-seeking not just in terms of *aspiration* but also in terms of *action*. Thomas Aquinas wrote that the resort to force, or threat of force, should focus attention on three objectives: order, justice, and peace.[2] Order is providing enduring security and stability for all parties, the function that Romans 13 describes government filling. Justice should motivate government action to right past wrongs, prevent future wrongdoing, punish wrongdoers (including among our own troops), and provide, when possible, some restitution to victims. The fruit of justice is peace. Order and justice, therefore, are the foundations for an enduring peace among citizens and among nations. Such a political peace can provide the basis for deepening bonds of conciliatory relationships and the pursuit of common goods, such as diplomatic and economic relations, over time. In chapters 1 and 2 I have discussed theory and theology. This chapter looks at application: How have the proponents of just war statecraft applied their criteria to real-world security dilemmas? Building on the discussion of peace in chapter 1, this chapter considers how Christian just war thinkers over two millennia have applied just war criteria to specific security dilemmas, such as the following:

- military service in the Roman Empire
- how to be a Christian citizen in both the world of human beings and the city of God
- the responsibility of government to provide peace
- the rights and protection of noncombatants in time of war
- the role of leaders in protecting civilians from tyranny
- contemporary issues such as weapons of mass destruction and armed humanitarian intervention

The good news is that great Christian minds have been dealing with these issues for two millennia. We have much to learn from them about how to promote responsible action by government authorities to deter and punish evil assaults on the order of society, restrain the destructiveness of warfare, and work toward a better state of peace.

Peace and the Question of Pacifism in the Early Church

There is a common misperception that the early church was pacifist due to Christ's "turn the other cheek" teaching and the low social status of many early Christians. However, as evangelical scholars J. Daryl Charles, Timothy Demy, and others have convincingly documented, Christian history provides no evidence that the early church took a unified pacifist position. Although many second- and third-century Christians were deeply skeptical of employment in Rome's armies,[3] John the Baptist, Jesus, Peter, and Paul all engage directly with tax collectors, soldiers, and Roman public officials without deriding their professions or their expertise.

New Testament leaders, including Christ, never suggest that soldiers or other public servants quit their work. John the Baptist instructed soldiers to avoid abusing their power and be content with their wages (Luke 3:14). Jesus said that a Roman centurion had the greatest faith in Israel (Matt. 8:10). Peter's first gentile convert was a Roman centurion with his family, a man who was already a devout seeker of God (Acts 10). C. S. Lewis captured the New Testament just war ethic in his critique of pacifism: "It harmonizes better with St. John the Baptist's words to the soldier and with the fact that one of the few persons whom Our Lord praised without reservation was a Roman centurion. It also allows me to suppose that the New Testament is consistent with itself. St. Paul approves of the magistrate's use of the sword (Romans 13:4) and so does St. Peter (1 Peter 2:14)."[4]

Nevertheless, many Christians had compelling reservations against serving the political authority of the day, which was Rome.[5] Christians, like Jews, rejected the idolatry and emperor cult of Rome and were persecuted by taxation and later imprisonment, crucifixion, and martyrdom in the arena. A good illustration of what the church was teaching at that time can be seen in Acts 15—the instruction that the Jerusalem Council gives to newly converted gentiles. New Christians were expected to abide by the basic moral law of the Old Testament: the Ten Commandments as summarized in loving God and loving one's neighbor as oneself based upon Jesus's teaching. Must gentile followers of "the Way" also undergo circumcision and live by the ceremonial obligations of Old Testament Jewish law? No, the council decides. But gentile converts should avoid meat offered to idols and abstain from sexual immorality. Why these two? First, food offered to idols was suggestive of the many ways that pagan religious practices were a part of the Greco-Roman world, including sacred oaths to the emperor and the ritual sacrifice of animals that later ended up in butchers' stalls. By refusing to eat this sacrificial food, Christians would avoid practicing or reinforcing idol worship. Second, sexual morality is the fundamental basis for the purity of the family and thus a building block for God's design for society. In the Roman and Near Eastern world, sexual promiscuity was not only rampant but encouraged. Some temples had cultic prostitutes, both male and female, and many politico-religious ceremonies disintegrated into debauchery and sexual immorality.

Furthermore, for those serving in the Roman army, there were severe restrictions on marriage. Roman military tradition, codified by Caesar Augustus, made it virtually illegal to marry if one served in the legions (legionaries could not legally marry until they had served a decade or more).[6] This encouraged prostitution just outside the camp gates and led to rape of the defeated as common practice in Roman warfare. When in garrison, legionaries took common-law wives. The women and their children were typically abandoned when the soldiers were assigned to a new posting.

The Jerusalem Council's instruction to gentile converts to avoid meat offered to idols and sexual promiscuity would have targeted these immoral practices that occurred, among other places, in public service and military roles. The church sought to avoid these corrupting practices, but it did not pronounce pacifist principles.[7]

The writings of the early church father Tertullian (155–220), while not entirely consistent, are a case in point. Tertullian's *On Idolatry* and parts of his *Apology* make it seem impossible for the soldier to be a Christian, due primarily to the idolatry and immorality discussed above. But elsewhere Tertullian commends Christians in the military. His *Apology* describes a famous episode, recounted by others including Emperor Marcus Aurelius (121–80) and the historian Eusebius (ca. 260–339), when Christian legionaries in the Twelfth Legion knelt and prayed for rain during a terrible drought. Lightning from heaven scared off the enemy troops and rain provided desperately needed water for what became known as the "Thundering Legion."[8] Tertullian wrote a later work called "On the Military Crown," which cogently discusses the vital place of service and the challenges of idolatry faced by Christian magistrates and soldiers. Another influential early church father, Origen (185–254), points to the service of Christians in the military as a sign that Christians did not seek the downfall of the Roman government; so do Eusebius and Augustine at later dates. In other words, Christians, as loyal citizens, are not to be confused with the rebellious Jews and their cycle of vicious revolts: Christians are not going to attempt to overthrow the civic peace of the Pax Romana. Origen allows that there are some righteous causes and it is just to defend one's country, though he is skeptical that Christians in such roles could keep themselves entirely free from Roman idolatry.[9]

Over time an argument did develop within Christianity for what can be called "professional pacifism" as theologians differentiated between the citizen's duty to the state, including military service, and the pacific duties of the churchman.[10] In other words, those living the spiritual vocation (pastors, monks, priests) were generally not to take up arms, but that did not mean that government was to leave them unprotected, nor did it mean that their parishioners should abstain from protecting their fellow citizens. Augustine famously makes this point in a letter to a Roman military officer named Boniface.[11] Augustine exhorts Boniface to fulfill his calling and fight against temporal enemies who seek to destroy the peace, while distinguishing it from the clergy's vocation of spiritual warfare: "Some, then, in praying for you, fight against your invisible enemies; you, in fighting for them, contend against the barbarians, their visible enemies."[12] Those enemies threatened the civic peace. In sum, whether in prayer or on the battlefield, different Christian vocations were working complementarily toward a peaceful end.

The Late Roman Empire and Augustine's "Tranquility of Order"

Augustine (354–430) is one of the most important Christian theologians in the history of the church. He is respected by Roman Catholics, Eastern Orthodox, and Protestants. His corpus of letters, pamphlets, books, and especially his magnum opus, *The City of God*, which deals with questions of life, law, politics, and peace, is massive and compelling. It is noteworthy that Augustine was writing during the last gasp of the Roman Empire. During his lifetime Rome was sacked by Alaric's Visigoths (AD 410), and Augustine died while his beloved city of Hippo, in modern-day Algeria, was under siege by the Vandals.

In book 19 of *The City of God*, Augustine provides an important explanation for how Christians ought to think about the perfect heavenly kingdom and their role as citizens in the limited, fallen world that they inhabit.[13] The kingdom of heaven ("city of God") is a place of perfect order and justice based on the perfect implementation of God's design and the active obedience of his subjects. The celestial city is characterized by perfect love. In contrast, earthly society—constituting Augustine's "city of man"—has all of the problems associated with the individual and collective fall of humankind, and thus is driven by self-love. Earthly government has the responsibility to promote the good and deter or punish evil, but the city of man is fallen and limited and, therefore, can at best only approximate the matchless good of the celestial city.

Augustine observes that every war is carried out with some view of peace, even if it is to be a cruel and rapacious victor's peace. In *The City of God* book 19, he writes,

> It is therefore with the desire for peace that wars are waged, even by those who take pleasure in exercising their warlike nature in command and battle. And hence it is obvious that peace is the end sought for by war. For every man seeks peace by waging war, but no man seeks war by making peace. For even they who intentionally interrupt the peace in which they are living have no hatred of peace, but only wish it changed into a peace that suits them better. They do not, therefore, wish to have no peace, but only one more to their mind.[14]

But Augustine writes that there is an ethical form of political peace that is possible in a fallen world, and he calls it the "tranquility of order." Peace, in this view, is experienced in a rightly ordered society that focuses on the security and justice of its citizens. That includes protecting their rights and livelihoods from the attacks of criminals and foreign adversaries. A mighty and just government can provide a high level of tranquil order to its people by ensuring justice and security. Thus, when it comes to international security, it is important to have not just a system of rights and laws but also the power to deter and defeat those who would disrupt the peace.[15]

He writes that "true religion looks upon as peaceful those wars that are waged not for motives of aggrandizement, or cruelty, but with the object of securing peace, of punishing evil-doers, and of uplifting the good."[16] For Augustine, the law of love includes both elements of justice: punishment that brings consequences for immoral behavior and restitution to right past wrongs.

Augustine's formulation of the just use of force relies heavily on the notion of "love" as rendered in Jesus's teaching on neighbor-love. In domestic society as well as international life, how does one go about loving one's neighbor? Augustine argues that within society adherence to the rule of law, including punishment of lawbreakers, is a way of loving one's neighbors. To love one's neighbors is to refrain from harming them and to support the authorities in their efforts to provide security for citizens. Moreover, Augustine notes, neighbor-love means protecting one's neighbor when he or she is attacked, even if that requires the use of force to protect the neighbor. Augustine cites Romans 13:1–5 in his argument that sovereign authorities have a responsibility to order and to justice, including the use of the sword:

> Let every person be subject to the governing authorities. For there is no authority except from God, and those that exist have been instituted by God. Therefore whoever resists the authorities resists what God has appointed, and those who resist will incur judgment. For rulers are not a terror to good conduct, but to bad. Would you have no fear of the one who is in authority? Then do what is good, and you will receive his approval, for he is God's servant for your good. But if you do wrong, be afraid, for he does not bear the sword in vain. For he is the servant of God, an avenger who carries out God's wrath on the wrongdoer. Therefore one must be in subjection, not only to avoid God's wrath but also for the sake of conscience.

Augustine suggests that this is also true with regard to foreign threats: loving our neighbor can mean self-defense of the polity. Likewise, loving our foreign neighbors may mean using force to punish evildoers or right a wrong.[17]

During his lifetime Augustine witnessed the alternative: the breakdown of the Pax Romana, the looting of Rome, and ultimately the sacking of his home in North Africa in the final days of his life. Augustine's fear of political disorder was more than a distaste for regime change. It was dread of losing civic order and the relative good it served for all humanity, including Christians. At the same time, what was most likely to follow the breakdown of law and order was, ultimately, the imposition of an unjust peace by a victorious but iniquitous ruler. Augustine goes on to write a passage that could be applied to rulers portrayed in *The Hunger Games* or Hitler's Third

Reich. An iniquitous ruler "hates equality with partners under God, but wants to impose its own domination upon its partners in place of God. Consequently, it hates the just peace of God and loves its own iniquitous peace. . . . The peace of the iniquitous, in comparison to the peace of the just, should not be called 'peace' at all."[18]

Thomas Aquinas on Authority, Just Cause, and Right Intention

Fifty years after Augustine's death, the Germanic chieftain Odoacer deposed the last Western Roman emperor (476), thus inaugurating what has long been called the Dark Ages, extending from roughly the fifth through the tenth centuries. As the Western Roman Empire fell apart, it was looted and divided up by European barbarians known as the Goths, Vandals, and Visigoths, and then, after 632, it came under assault by Islamic armies from Arabia. Within just one hundred years, those Muslim armies conquered the old Roman provinces of North Africa, including Augustine's Hippo, and much of the Iberian Peninsula before the tide was halted in 732 by Charles Martel near Tours, France. Muslim armies continued to attack the Eastern Roman Empire, based in Constantinople, for the next five hundred years and attacked Eastern Europe all the way to Vienna as late as 1683.

It is in this context that Thomas Aquinas (1225–74), the greatest Christian scholar of the Middle Ages and an important expositor of Augustine, writes. In the century before his birth, a number of counter-Islamic military campaigns, called the Crusades, were launched. These wars can best be understood as geopolitical reactions to the Islamic conquests of the previous three centuries. Aquinas's lifetime was a time of global warfare, with Mongol armies attacking from Japan to Eastern Europe, conquering Moscow, Kyiv, and countless other cities. There was war across the Mediterranean, including the sacking of Jerusalem by a Muslim army, and Europeans were fighting with one another in Scandinavia, Britain, and across the continent.

Thus, after the shattering of the Western Roman Empire, Eurasia continued to see leaders attempting to impose a new order and build new realms. It is against this backdrop that Aquinas briefly discusses peace and justice in his massive theological compendium, *Summa Theologica*. Looking at the disorder of the time and the competing claims of political legitimacy that were usually based on the power of the sword, Aquinas argues that might does not make right. Rather, the purpose of Christian statecraft is to provide order, justice, and peace. When force is needed to deter, punish, or protect, then the decision to use force should meet three requirements: it must be the decision of a sovereign authority, on the basis of a just cause, and with right intention. It is noteworthy that Aquinas begins not with just cause or right intention, but with legitimate political authority:

> In order for a war to be just, three things are necessary. First, the authority of the sovereign by whose command the war is to be waged. For it is not the business of a private individual to declare war. . . . And as the care of the common weal is committed to those who are in authority, it is their business to watch over the common weal of the city, kingdom or province subject to them. And just as it is lawful for them to have recourse to the sword in defending that common weal against internal disturbances, when they punish evil-doers . . . so too, it is their business to have recourse to the sword of war in defending the common weal against external enemies.[19]

In short, Aquinas sees violence as criminal and lawless. The fundamental purpose of government was to deter lawlessness. Only the rightful authorities may legitimately use force in order to promote security.

Aquinas also argues that governments should be concerned with just cause. He writes: "Secondly, a just cause is required, namely that those who are attacked, should be attacked because they deserve it on account of some fault."[20] He quotes Augustine: "A just war is wont to be described as one that avenges wrongs, when a nation or state has to be punished, for refusing to make amends for the wrongs inflicted by its subjects, or to restore what it has seized unjustly."[21] Aquinas's conception of just cause is richer than mere self-defense because it rightly emphasizes *justice* as indispensable to peacemaking: punishing wrongdoers and providing restitution of some sort to victims. Aquinas's just cause supports the use of force to curb aggressive criminals and terrorists and punish rogue regimes that disrupt international relations.

Third, Aquinas says that the just resort to force requires right intention: "Thirdly, it is necessary that the belligerents should have a rightful intention, so that they intend the advancement of good, or the avoidance of evil."[22] In other words, Aquinas's idea of right intention is that governments should seek to advance the security of their people and avoid wars based only on greed or vengeance. Aquinas again cites Augustine: "The passion for inflicting harm, the cruel thirst for vengeance, an unpacific and relentless spirit, the fever of revolt, the lust of power, and such like things, all these are rightly condemned in war."[23]

These three criteria—legitimate authority, just cause, and right intention—are the basis for Christian just war statecraft to actively promote peace to this very day. Moreover, the secular version of these principles has been codified in international law, such as in the principles of national sovereignty and nonintervention into the matters of another country. These principles appear in the United Nations Charter, which states that the only lawful causes for warfare have to do with violations of peace, such as infringements on the sovereignty and security of a country. Such lawful warfare would include the self-defense of one's own country, one's allies, or a victimized people group, including humanitarian intervention to stop genocide.

Vitoria and Restraining the Destructiveness of War

Francesco de Vitoria (1486–1546) was a Dominican friar educated at the University of Paris. He was famous throughout Europe for his wisdom and brilliant lectures at the University of Salamanca, and he was regularly consulted by political figures, including Holy Roman Emperor Charles V. He is one of a number of theologians, including Bartolomé de las Casas, Gabriel Vázquez, Francisco Suárez, and Luis de Molina, who responded to the warfare of the fifteenth and sixteenth centuries, providing us with the foundation for how we think about securing peace with restraint: by limiting how war is fought. This brings us to the category of *jus in bello*, the morality of warfighting.

Vitoria wrote at length about three major international crises of his day. The first of these concerns the defensive posture of Eastern European Christian countries facing the continuing onslaught of the Ottoman Turks. Muslim Ottoman armies conquered large swaths of Eastern Europe during this time, including parts of Hungary, Serbia, Bosnia, Herzegovina, Albania, Italy, various Mediterranean islands, and more. Vitoria writes that self-defense, of one's country and one's faith, by European monarchs is legitimate.

A second issue that Vitoria deals with is feuds within Christendom—notably, the ongoing violence between Spain and France. Vitoria condemns these ruptures of the peace of Christendom, which was Europe's shared Christian civilization, because they are motivated by dynastic struggles for land, wealth, and power rather than justice.

Vitoria's lasting contribution comes in his lengthy examination of the wars in the New World. At the time, small bands of Spanish and Portuguese soldiers were in conflict with the massive, wealthy empires in South and Central America. Vitoria recognized that this was not a novel situation but, rather, another example of two empires confronting one another on the world stage, just as the Ottomans, Mongols, and others had clashed with the great European empires in Russia, Venice, France, and Spain. Vitoria begins with the classic just war framework, that such wars could be just if fought by legitimate authorities with right intention on behalf of a just cause. At the time, the cause and intentions were clearly mixed, from exploration and evangelism to legitimate trade to outright greed. We see how complex the state of affairs was when we observe that in 1521 Hernán

Cortéz and his band of just a few hundred adventurers successfully allied with oppressed groups, like the Tlaxcalans, against the mighty Aztec Empire.

Over the next century, Vitoria and his colleagues dealt with two crucial issues. The first had to do with the justice of Europeans fighting against the Incas, Aztecs, and others in the first place. Some, such as Juan Ginés de Sepulveda, argued that it was morally right to conquer the native peoples because they had few natural rights as barbarians. The practices of human sacrifice and cannibalism, which were well documented even by the native peoples' defenders, suggested to many in Europe that the Indigenous peoples were subhuman and perhaps not even capable of full intellectual development, much less Christian salvation. The harder-edged version of this view, influenced by Aristotle, defined the native peoples as barbaric to the point of being nonhuman. The softer version, like that of Sepulveda, argued that it was just to conquer the opposing kingdoms and make the inhabitants develop their rational capabilities under Spanish tutelage.

Vitoria and others vehemently disagreed with this analysis, arguing for the humanity of all involved and reiterating the just war framework as the appropriate way for thinking about when it is licit for governments to go to war. Vitoria's argument is a critical assertion of human dignity based on the fact that God created all people in his image, the doctrine of the *imago Dei*. Vitoria provided an indispensable part of the foundation of the modern conception of universal human rights.

A second major controversy Vitoria deals with is the methodology of warfare. Vitoria asserts that the struggle between governments and armies should happen via diplomacy and on the battlefield, not through the widespread destruction and plundering of the civilian population and private property. Vitoria calls such devastation *sinful*. It is wrong to kill noncombatants such as women, children, "harmless agricultural folk," "clerics and members of religious orders," and even enemy prisoners who are no longer a threat. Vitoria writes,

"The reason for this restriction is clear: for these persons are innocent, neither is it needful to the attainment of victory that they should be slain. It would be heretical to say that it is licit to kill them. . . . Accordingly, the innocent may not be slain by (primary) intent, when it is possible to distinguish them from the guilty."[24] The moral worth of human beings was clearly at stake. In addition to that, when the basic infrastructure of society, such as agriculture, wells, and homes, is devastated, it is far harder to quickly return to the basic pursuits of human subsistence and peace. Vitoria observes that Deuteronomy 12 provides a number of limits on warfare, including magnanimity to those who surrender (v. 10) and the protection of agriculture (vv. 19–20). Vitoria cites Aquinas's emphasis that the purpose of government was to advance order, justice, and peace. Vitoria's principle of protecting noncombatants and their subsistence is now codified in international law.

Pursuing Peace during the Reformation

By the time of the Reformation, Christians had developed fifteen hundred years of biblical reflection on the issues of statecraft and peace. Luther, Calvin, Knox, and other key Reformers were most concerned with the biblical justification for the proper and constrained role of government due to the intertwining of the papacy and politics for the previous thousand years. Luther and Calvin wrote extensive commentaries on the Scripture, and thus dealt with everything from the leadership legacy of King David to applying the teaching of Romans 13 on the citizen's duty to government. By the Reformation, the building blocks of just war statecraft, particularly key scriptural passages and exemplars, as well as the unfolding of the applied tradition in the works of Augustine, Aquinas, and others, were well established and embraced by the Reformers. Indeed, Calvin and Luther routinely cited Aquinas and, especially, Augustine. This history is well cataloged in a number of books by Christian scholars such as James Turner Johnson, David Corey, Timothy Demy, and J. Daryl Charles,

some of which are referenced in the suggested reading list at the end
of this book.

There are, however, two variants that arose during the Reformation that debated how to think about the responsibility to protect and
promote civic peace. The first of these is the Anabaptist position—
developed in the sixteenth century—that Christians may *not* serve
in public office and therefore never participate in the judiciary, law
enforcement, or the military. The second, often associated with John
Knox and the Reformed and Presbyterian tradition, is the innovation
that *intermediate authorities* or lesser magistrates have a responsibility to promote domestic tranquility and justice, even if it means using
force to protect the citizens in their charge from tyrannical overlords.

The Radical Reformation—Anabaptists

One splinter group from the Reformation is Anabaptism (not to
be confused with today's Baptists), and its line of thinking about
war is the foundation for a narrow form of Christian pacifism in the
modern era.[25] To this day, only a tiny minority of Christians associ-
ate with Anabaptism. The foundational statement of the Anabaptist
movement is the Schleitheim Confession of 1527. Schleitheim made
three key points in response to the teaching of Romans 13 that "the
ruler wields the sword for your good."

1. The "use of the sword" is "ordained by God" but "outside the
   perfection of Christ." Thus it is appropriate for "worldly magistrates" to "punish," "put to death the wicked," and "guard and
   protect the good." Within the church, however, the strongest
   use of force is "the ban" (excommunication).

2. Just as "Christ was meek and lowly," it is not appropriate for
   Christians to "employ the sword against the wicked for the
   defense and protection of the good." Christians should not
   take any job that would require them to employ force, such as
   law enforcement or military, nor should they take an office like

that of a judge or certain political positions that would require them to make judgments between unbelievers.

3. Christians should pray for those in worldly authority because those individuals do the important work of limiting evil in a fallen world. But Christians should not participate.[26]

Classic Anabaptist pacifism says that the Christian should pray for those who restrain evil but should not participate in public service because it will dirty one's hands and nullify the witness of the believer. Anabaptists do not believe that in the New Testament era God would call some Christians to serve in public office. They believe a Christian's responsibility to protect their fellow human beings is limited to prayer, witness, and forms of humanitarian service. In practice Anabaptism has been rightly criticized as irresponsible for not engaging civic life and avoiding important political responsibilities. Today, practicing Anabaptists make up only a tiny minority of Christians, such as in the Amish, Mennonite, Hutterite, and similar communities. A form of pacifism later became fashionable among some protestors of the Vietnam War, but it was typically thin on theological grounding and quite different from the theology of Schleitheim.

More will be said later about variants of pacifism that rely on personal feelings, a preference to avoid the mess of political life, vague sentiments of solidarity with the vulnerable, a lack of responsibility to protect, and the like. But at the end of the day, the Anabaptist model has not been embraced by the majority of Christians over the past two millennia because it denies doctrines of active neighbor-love via vocations of public service and stewardship. Indeed, when we think about Christian heroes such as William Wilberforce, who led the fight against the slave trade in the British Parliament; Abraham Kuyper, who modeled a Christian engagement in politics while serving as prime minister in the Netherlands; or Christians motivated to protect their neighbors, stop genocide, and shutter concentration camps, we can conclude that just war statecraft was not just for Moses, Hezekiah, and Nehemiah, but is an honorable and necessary calling today. As Dietrich Bonhoeffer (1906–45), who was martyred by the Nazis for his involvement in a plot to stop Hitler, concluded: "If we want to be Christians, we must have some share in Christ's large-heartedness by acting with responsibility and in freedom when the hour of danger comes. . . . Mere waiting and looking on is not Christian behavior."[27]

Calvin and the Reformed Tradition on Resisting Tyranny

Underlying any discussion of societal peace are two issues. First, what responsibility do citizens have to obey the government, even an illegitimate or immoral government? Second, what responsibility do government officials have when faced with immoral or unlawful orders from their superiors? One can see how Aquinas's two forms of peace might be at odds here. I may be ordered by government authority to act against God's law. In other words, the external peace associated with submission to government authority may actually violate the internal peace of my soul. What is to be done?

In general, Christian citizens are to obey government authorities, even when under wicked governments. Luther and Calvin affirmed this numerous times, even during the chaotic years of the Reformation. However, there are times when such obedience to temporal authorities would be a sin. The issue at hand is this: When is it appropriate to obey odious earthly authorities and when is it proper to disobey or resist? Augustine, Calvin, and others looked to biblical examples for how to respond in these scenarios.

First, it should be noted that Christians have been united in saying that when persecuted for the Christian faith, one should not renounce Christ, even to the point of martyrdom. Shadrach, Meshach, Abednego (Dan. 3), and Daniel (Dan. 6) all refuse to deny their faith, even though they are government officials facing not just loss of position but loss of their very lives. Esther risks death by breaking convention and approaching the king (Esther 5). New Testament martyrs such as Stephen and Paul are killed for their professions of faith.

But Daniel and the others were able to live most of their lives peacefully under these wicked regimes, and it is extremely rare for the Christian to be in a life-or-death moment for their profession of Christ. What is far more likely is a citizen being ordered to participate in a sin. This is a different matter from renouncing Christ. Augustine and later Calvin approvingly cite the civil disobedience of the Hebrew midwives (Exod. 1) who not only disobey Pharaoh but also lie to cover up their willful noncompliance when called upon to murder innocent Hebrew babies. The midwives' first allegiance was to God, not to government edict. Calvin, reflecting on this incident, writes that Christians are obligated to avoid complying with "the impious and wicked edicts of Kings," because those who do so "display by their cowardice an inexcusable contempt for God."[28] The same moral logic applies to average citizens who hid Jews in their basements and deceived the Nazis. As we will see in chapter 4, these citizens were obeying God's higher law to love their neighbors and not be implicated in the murder of the Jews. To uphold God's law, they had to violate a lesser, man-made law.

Calvin routinely emphasizes that Christian *citizens* should generally endure with patience the situation of living in an unjust and immoral political environment. However, do *political officials* have a different responsibility than private citizens when it comes to obeying orders? Calvin and others assert that at times it is appropriate to resist government tyranny and that the people who have the chief responsibility to do so are not private citizens but rather intermediate or midlevel authorities, or lesser magistrates, as Calvin calls them. In other words, a mayor or governor should protect the people in their charge against a tyrannical king or president or prime minister. Over time, theories of resistance were debated among Calvinist thinkers such as John Knox, Peter Martyr Vermigli, and Theodore Beza.[29] This was not merely a theoretical debate, because in France and Britain Protestants could be tortured and burned at the stake for their faith. Perhaps the most important work from this era is John Ponet's *A Short Treatise on Political Power*, which explored the moral foundations of government and argued that resistance is justified—even morally required in some cases—if the national political authority has become corrupt and tyrannical.

The argument for intermediate authorities protecting citizens within their charge from tyrannical rulers actually goes all the way back to Aquinas, who writes in *On Kingship*, "To proceed against the cruelty of tyrants is an action to be undertaken, not through private presumption of the few, but rather by public authority."[30] Aquinas argues, "If to provide itself with a king belongs to the right of a given multitude, it is not unjust that the king be deposed or have his power restricted by the same multitude, if, becoming a tyrant, he abuses the royal power." Elsewhere Aquinas provides a very narrow argument for tyrannicide based on his previous arguments for capital punishment and just war: "He who kills a tyrant (i.e., a usurper) to free his country is praised and rewarded."[31] Calvin goes on to explain the responsibility and appropriate motivations for such action.

> For if there are now any magistrates of the people, appointed to restrain the willfulness of kings (as in ancient times the ephors were set against the Spartan kings, or the tribunes of the people against the Roman consuls, or the demarchs against the senate of the Athenians; and perhaps, as things now are, such power as the three estates exercise in every realm when they hold their chief assemblies), I am so far from forbidding them to withstand, in accordance with their duty, the fierce licentiousness of kings, that, if they wink at kings who violently fall upon and assault the lowly common folk, I declare that their dissimulation involves nefarious perfidy, because they dishonestly betray the freedom of the people, of which they know that they have been appointed protectors by God's ordinance.[32]

In sum, one important way of thinking about peace is to consider how to maintain social harmony and justice, particularly in situations of increasingly immoral regulations imposed by a tyrannical ruler, such as a Hitler or a Stalin. The foundations for this type of Christian thinking were laid during the Reformation in Europe and in

Scotland and, as we will see in chapter 4, had a very direct influence on both the American War for Independence and the underlying logic of Martin Luther King Jr.'s civil disobedience campaign.

Paul Ramsey: Applying Neighbor-Love to Nuclear Deterrence

A discussion of nuclear deterrence may not seem to belong in a chapter on peace. It is included here to demonstrate, first, how a Christian expert contributed to national debates of great significance and, second, that a political ethic of responsible neighbor-love applies even when one is considering the direst aspects of armed conflict. Christian ethicist Paul Ramsey (1913–88) contributed to our moral thinking on this debate in two ways: first, by *not* advocating the abolition of such weapons, which would have put America at risk of nuclear blackmail, and second, by articulating important moral limits on Western nuclear strategy.

After World War II, a number of Christian voices contended, just as in the 1920s, that war had become so destructive that it was *always* immoral. The advent of atomic weapons seemed to strengthen their case. However, when one looks at the brazen advancement of the Soviet military in Asia and Eastern Europe from 1945 to 1948, one can only wonder how a pacifist response would have stopped further Communist aggression. One part of the West's response to the massive Soviet buildup in Eastern Europe was investment in nuclear weapons. With the danger of nuclear holocaust in mind, Ramsey was most interested in a realistic peace that would limit the likelihood of hot war between the Soviet Union and NATO. He argued that nuclear deterrence, due to the ambiguity of our intentions and the nature of nuclear power, was a crucial preventive to additional Soviet aggression, particularly in Europe and North America. In other words, Ramsey advocated a responsible "peace through strength," as President Reagan would later call for, or, as Roman general Vegetius said, "If you want peace, prepare for war." Careful preparation of a nuclear deterrent allowed for a good deal of peace for the American people and their democratic allies in the West. Nuclear deterrence forestalled World War III.

However, Ramsey went on to argue, we must also express our limits, and those limits are rooted in our love of humanity. Even our erstwhile enemies in the Soviet Union, the Russian people, are our "neighbors." How do we love our neighbors when faced by an aggressive bully like the Soviet Union, whose leader bragged, "We will bury you," to Western and Israeli diplomats? How do we love our neighbors in a time of nuclear deterrence? According to Ramsey, government officials are responsible to love their own citizens by thoughtful and robust self-defense measures. We also love our neighbors by fulfilling our treaty obligations to our allies. Importantly, when it comes to nuclear weapons, we demonstrate neighbor-love by pledging to never strike first, but only to respond to an attack by our enemies. Ramsey went on to assert that we love our neighbor by pledging only to target military bases and personnel rather than cities and populations.

Far more could be said, but one can see that Ramsey is trying to protect the "tranquility of order" in the city of man by a sophisticated and tough strategy of nuclear deterrence. From Tertullian and Augustine to Ramsey, there is a genealogy of just war statecraft that has as its primary focus the concept of securing and maintaining some form of peaceful order in a dangerous and fallen world.

Neighbor-Love and Armed Humanitarian Intervention

A final contemporary issue is that of armed humanitarian intervention, the imposition of military force by an external government or coalition, usually to stop some form of crimes against humanity. After the end of the Cold War (1991), United Nations and NATO-authorized armed interventions have taken place in response to the bloody events in Iraq, Rwanda, Bosnia, Congo, East Timor, Kosovo, and elsewhere. Many Christian scholars have responded to these events in the popular press and academic works, such as George Weigel, Jean Bethke Elshtain, Keith Pavlischek, J. Daryl Charles, and others.

The great anti-Communist pope, John Paul II, called armed humanitarian intervention by outside governments "obligatory . . . where the survival of populations and entire ethnic groups is seriously compromised." Under such circumstances, the pope saw it as "a duty for nations and the international community."[33] The argument here is similar to one Ramsey made in the 1960s, that all governments share a responsibility to uphold human rights in international life. Other religious leaders agreed, "The forceful, direct intervention by one or more states or international organizations in the internal affairs of other states for essentially humanitarian purposes," including alleviating "internal chaos, repression and widespread loss of life," is just. The aim of such intervention is "to protect human life and basic human rights" in such contexts.[34] International legal principles of sovereignty and nonintervention do not allow governments carte blanche to massacre their own citizens: "Nevertheless, [considering] populations who are succumbing to the attacks of an unjust aggressor, states no longer have a 'right to indifference.' It seems clear that their duty is to disarm the aggressor if all other means have proved ineffective. The principles of sovereignty of states and of noninterference in their internal affairs cannot constitute a screen behind which torture and murder may be carried out."[35]

Jean Bethke Elshtain (1941–2013) argues that the Christian concept of love of neighbor can be expressed in international relations by the principle of "equal regard": we regard all people everywhere as human beings with fundamental rights to live and thrive. Even if we cannot always do something to protect them and we never interact with them, they have moral worth and dignity equal to our own, and all governments must recognize this fact. People are not just statistics, and our posture toward them should be based on the Golden Rule.[36] J. Daryl Charles (1950–) takes a similar approach, arguing that governments have a moral responsibility to consider whether to intervene in cases of gross injustice and crimes against humanity.

Governments may decide, for a number of reasons, whether or not to intervene militarily, but they are duty-bound under international law and basic morality to consider how to protect all of God's children.[37]

Does this mean, however, that we are obligated to act in *all times* and in *all places* where there is injustice? Charles argues that we must be very careful not to exacerbate a bad situation, making it worse. We must carefully consider the possible unintended consequences of deploying military force to places such as Somalia and Iraq. Charles also cites an argument made by Ramsey a generation earlier: "What needs morally to be done in the world always requires resources far greater than those available. The statesman . . . is not called to office to aim at all the humanitarian good that can be aimed at in the world. Instead he must determine what he ought to do from out of the total humanitarian that ought to be."[38] This is reminiscent of C. S. Lewis's consideration of love in *The Four Loves*. Each of us has concentric circles of responsibility that begin with our immediate family and neighborhood and expand to our community, and then larger and more ambiguous communities such as nations around the globe. We, as individuals or as governments, simply cannot exercise the same level of loving responsibility to those far off as we do to those whom God has entrusted to our immediate care. Consequently, wise statecraft involves carefully considered choices among the possibilities for moral action.[39] It is an abrogation of neighbor-love to avoid consideration of the range of potential choices when faced with global crises, even if the options for direct action are limited.

Conclusion: The Problem with Pacifism

The purpose of this chapter is to demonstrate the hard work that Christian theologians and scholars have done in attempting to apply an ethic of responsible neighbor-love to the challenges of peace and security in a fallen world. Many call this approach "Augustinian Realism" or "Christian Realism" in order to distinguish it from forms of "Christian Idealism" that do not adequately reckon with circumstances in a fallen world.

This brings us, in conclusion, to some of the problems of pacifism. Few pacifists are truly absolute pacifists, when pacifism is defined in terms of consistent moral opposition to the use of force in each and every case. In reality, today's pacifism is typically a sloppy quasi-pacifism. Most so-called pacifists do not know anything about the Schleitheim Confession, nor can they articulate a scriptural and theological justification for a pacifism that makes them, and their governments, not responsible in cases of local violence or ugly international instances of genocide, ethnic cleansing, and crimes against humanity.

Let's take a closer look. There are at least two mistakes that people make when thinking about pacifism. The first is to consider the responsibility of an *individual citizen* precisely the same as that of a *government official*. The second is not distinguishing *force* from *violence*.

True, the Bible has a lot to say about individual Christians being agents for peace as private citizens. We are admonished to be peacemakers: "Do good to those who hate you" (Luke 6:27). "Do not resist the one who is evil. . . . Turn to him the other [cheek] also" (Matt. 5:39). "Never avenge yourselves" (Rom. 12:19). All of these exhortations take place at the level of the individual person. It is important to realize that we can analyze moral action at three different levels of human interaction. Beyond the individual is a second level, that of domestic society, which includes the social life of communities, churches, Rotary clubs, softball leagues, elections and national politics, and all else that we share as American citizens governed by the Constitution and other US laws. We can also examine a third level: international affairs. This level is primarily defined by how governments interact with one another on the global stage. When studying war, peace, and security, we must recognize a difference between what happens between neighbors and what happens between governments.

"Turn the other cheek" is appropriate in interpersonal relations, and it is a good reminder for all people, including government officials, to have patience. C. S. Lewis addressed turning the other cheek at Oxford in 1940. He reminded his audience that since Jesus's context was an "audience of private people in a disarmed nation, it seems unlikely that they would have ever supposed Our Lord to be referring to war. War was not what they would have been thinking of. The frictions of daily life among villagers were more likely to be in their minds."[40]

However, when considering domestic society and international affairs, people serving in government have a responsibility to act in accord with the teaching of Romans 13, which enjoins leaders to enforce the law for the common good of all citizens. Police officers and soldiers, when on duty, are not to turn the other cheek to violent criminals but to act with restrained yet decisive force. When off duty, they have other roles to play as private citizens, taxpayers, and family members. In short, Christians need to avoid simplifying teaching on neighbor-love by failing to recognize the various ways it must be carried out at the level of the individual, the level of domestic society, and the international level.

The second misperception occurs when we fail to distinguish force from violence. Force can be lawful, restrained, right intentioned, and dispensed by lawful authority with an eye toward peace, justice, and security. In contrast, violence is unrestrained, lawless, and motivated by sinful desires such as bitterness, hatred, greed, and envy. We can tell the difference between loving but firm discipline and furious harshness. We can tell the difference between the limited use of lethal force to save victims and police brutality. We can also tell the difference between robust but restrained military force and vengeful killing, plunder, and devastation.

Getting these distinctions right helps Christians to recognize that biblical teaching on peace is multifaceted. We must take into account what it means to both live in peace with our next-door neighbor and keep the peace, the "tranquility of order," among millions of people. However, there is another reason that people fall into pacifism, and that is their unwillingness to think critically and act responsibly in times of controversy and insecurity.

At the outset of World War II, theologian Reinhold Niebuhr drafted an essay not unlike C. S. Lewis's "Why I Am Not a Pacifist." Niebuhr's was called "Why the Christian Church Is Not Pacifist." In that essay, and elsewhere, Niebuhr denounces the irresponsibility of those he calls "political pacifists." The problem was a pragmatic, rather than moral, pacifism that wrung its hands over the destruction of World War I and vainly hoped that somehow appeasing Hitler—by sacrificing the Czechs, Poles, and others—might somehow save our skins. This was compounded by numerous prominent American Christians self-righteously arguing that going to war in Europe in 1939–40 would be immoral because both sides, the British Empire and the Third Reich, were "empires" and, therefore, equally evil. Niebuhr responds that a mature, ethical person can tell the qualitative moral difference between Hitler's Nazism and British rule in Jamaica.[41] Niebuhr argues that political pacifists claim a form of "neutrality" that is conceited, irresponsible, and naive because it fails to recognize, or deliberately avoids, the fact that power struggles in human relations cannot be overcome by renunciation and good will.[42] Unlike the small number of *professional* pacifists—such as monks and nuns—who model Christ's life of self-abnegation, *political* pacifists refuse to make moral judgments about political categories.

Niebuhr and his Christian contemporaries, such as John C. Bennett, Martin Wight, and Herbert Butterfield, were also critical of the idealism of many Christian pacifists. In the first half of the twentieth century, there were a variety of idealistic impulses toward pacifism, blending traditional American isolationism and neutrality with varied religious sources: the "end times" eschatology of the burgeoning holiness and Pentecostal movements; the social perfectionism that undergirded social movements like abolition, temperance, women's rights; and political alliances between some mainline churches and church organizations with social actors such as organized labor. Niebuhr argues that we cannot simply renovate social institutions and educate humanity beyond the violent prejudice that causes gross inequality at home and conflict abroad. We have to rightly diagnose sin at the root of these problems and act vigilantly for a just peace, rather than for an iniquitous settlement. He writes,

> Whenever modern idealists are confronted with the divisive and corrosive effects of man's self love, they look for some immediate cause of this perennial tendency, usually in some specific form of social organization. One school holds that men would be good if only political institutions would not corrupt them, another believes that they would be good if the prior evil of a faulty economic organization could be eliminated. Or another school thinks of this evil as no more than ignorance, and therefore waits for a more perfect educational process to redeem man from his partial and particular loyalties. But no school asks how it is that an essentially good man could have produced corrupting and tyrannical political organizations or exploiting economic organizations or fanatical and superstitious religious organizations.[43]

To Niebuhr the obvious prescription for dealing with social evils is not a hope that education and good intentions will solve society's ills but rather countervailing force. Not surprisingly, Niebuhr was a longtime supporter of the civil rights movement, and he wrote about the important campaigns of labor unions, Gandhi, and Martin Luther King Jr. Niebuhr's principle of countervailing force also applies to the struggles with Nazi Germany, Imperial Japan, and, later, the Soviet Union.

What about "just peacemaking"? This is a catchy term, but a careful review of the writings of its advocates, such as the late Fuller Seminary professor Glen Stassen, exposes a very problematic perspective. Stassen rightly argues, as I will in chapter 6, that there are many roles that Christians can play to serve the interest of peace, from humanitarian work in failed states to serving as "Track 2 Diplomats"—that is, nonofficial intermediaries between belligerent powers. But even a cursory analysis of Stassen's writings shows a lack of moral clarity when it comes to actual war. Stassen advocates a militant pacifism, typically casting the United States as an imperialist aggressor. A case in point of this bizarre viewpoint is Stassen's analysis of the 1999

Kosovo campaign, during which the West intervened to stop ethnic cleansing in the Balkans at the hands of the diabolical Serbian regime that had murdered thousands of Muslims just five years earlier. Stassen advocated sending human shields to stop the war. What many do not realize is that Stassen wanted Westerners—Americans and Canadians and others—to go to Serbia and stand as human shields so that NATO would be unable to attack the vicious Serbian military as it moved into position to massacre civilians. He advocated blocking an armed humanitarian intervention that saved countless lives. Many rightly view this form of "nonviolence" as irresponsible: it is not "just peacemaking" to tacitly aid genocide.

Wasn't Martin Luther King Jr.'s "nonviolent direct action" a peaceful alternative to war? We will carefully look at King's important contributions in the next chapter, but a simple distinction is in order. King himself recognized that there are at least two models of disobedience that the moral person can employ when confronted by injustice, and those models are based, in large part, on context. King, following Gandhi, demanded the equal rights of all citizens within a democratic society. The national government had a constitution and laws that it was supposed to uphold, and it was also restrained by public opinion and its own legal system in the mid-twentieth century. The British in India and government authorities in the United States, despite bad intentions and true shortcomings, were not going to resort to concentration camps and genocide. Violent resistance, such as what Malcolm X demanded, was morally inappropriate and even counterproductive. However, King recognizes that the situation of someone like Dietrich Bonhoeffer in Nazi Germany was different and would require different forms of resistance. Bonhoeffer was right to voluntarily participate in a plot to assassinate Hitler and stop his regime's atrocities. It is to the moral reasoning behind resistance in such cases, expressed with particular elegance and sophistication in King's *Letter from Birmingham Jail*, that we now turn.

4

Morality and Contemporary Warfare

Distinguishing Moral Resistance from Violent Rebellion

Trumpet fanfares, the clash of swords, and grunting knights. These are the hallmarks of the 1975 cult classic *Monty Python and the Holy Grail*. The slapstick film resulted in many pop culture references, most notably that a grievous blow is "just a flesh wound." The scene in question takes place as Arthur, king of the Britons, and his squire come upon a desperate sword fight between opposing knights clad in black and green. After a lengthy demonstration of skilled swordsmanship, the Black Knight vanquishes his rival. King Arthur, always on the lookout for talent that can help expand the security provided by the brotherhood of the Round Table, engages the victor.

The Black Knight mutely ignores King Arthur's invitation to join the company of the Round Table. Arthur responds, "You make me sad. So be it." Willing to live and let live, Arthur and his squire prepare to cross the small bridge that the Black Knight seems to be obstruct-ing. It is at this moment that the Black Knight declares, "None shall pass!" The scene is famous for the battle between Arthur and the Black Knight, including the hilarious and completely unrealistic loss of the Black Knight's limbs one by one. It is at this point that the Black Knight says the wounds are only "a flesh wound," "a scratch," and claims, "I've had worse." At the end of the struggle the Black Knight demands Arthur come closer so that the former can "bite your legs off!"

Here is the question: What action should Arthur, king of the Brit-ons, have taken in dealing with the Black Knight? Would it have been appropriate to avoid conflict, for Arthur to slink away and seek another path to his destination? Should Arthur have, so to speak, turned the other cheek?

The answer is obviously no. Had Arthur been a *private citizen*, he might have been able to back away from a brigand, criminal, or terrorist operating in Britain. As *king*, however, Arthur is Britain's lawful authority—the living embodiment of the law and security of the realm—responsible in such cases to clear the roadways of brig-ands or bandits and to ensure that the commerce of peasants and merchants can continue. This means Arthur must fight against the Black Knight so that he and others can cross that bridge rather than traveling lengthy miles around it. By not fighting, Arthur would be forfeiting his solemn obligation as sovereign of the realm. The Black Knight is not merely a local thug, nor is he just a skilled warrior liv-ing as a law unto himself. Rather, the Black Knight is a threat to the tranquility of order: to law, justice, and security in British society. It is Arthur's sacred duty to curtail such a threat to public safety and commerce, even if he has to fight the Black Knight alone.

The rattlesnake nature of the Black Knight—who absurdly keeps struggling to kill even at the point of death—is an adequate portrait of many of the threats citizens face day to day around the world, par-ticularly those associated with the violent Islamism of Boko Haram, al Qaeda, and the so-called Islamic State (ISIS). Furthermore, a great deal of the violence in the South China Sea, the Middle East and Africa, or across the favelas and urban centers of Latin America is this type of lawlessness. Whether in the form of pirates, criminal cartels, or terrorists, each is an example of the way that violence is most likely to flourish where there is a lack of legitimate political authority upholding its responsibility to protect and serve their realms.

Just war statecraft begins with the responsibility that authorities have to promote order and justice; those who commit violence without that legitimate authority are dangers to the common good. This chapter looks at the moral issues in some of the most controversial situations of force and violence of recent years, with an eye toward making right distinctions and getting our categories correct. For instance, we will look at the way a mass movement of citizens focused on exercising their fundamental political rights *within* a political system may be forced to break unjust laws and suffer repression by unjust authorities. This is a critical issue of how the principles of authority, just cause, and right intentions come together within an oppressive system. In this vein, we will examine the inspiring ideas of Martin Luther King Jr. and his pragmatic approach to "nonviolent direct action" within a democracy. The US civil rights movement demonstrates that the just statecraft principles are applicable to domestic political authorities, the legal system, and law enforcement. In contrast to King, we will also look at those who lived in nondemocratic, totalitarian situations. Dietrich Bonhoeffer was one such individual, a German Christian pastor who refused to support the Nazis. Ultimately, Bonhoeffer was executed for his participation in a failed plot to knock Germany out of the war by assassinating Adolf Hitler—the head of the Third Reich's war machine.

We live in a time of moral equivocations, when some have suggested that one man's freedom fighter is another man's terrorist. Just statecraft principles are vital to help us make important distinctions. We need to differentiate ethical *resistance* from *armed rebellion* that degrades not just the human person but also societal flourishing. This will help us evaluate the moral depravity of today's terrorism and forms of so-called holy war, perhaps better labeled as a "religiously justified war," whose proponents typically assert that apocalyptic ends justify any violent means. Finally, we will look at elements of the American War for Independence and how it demonstrates the just statecraft principles of *legitimate authority*, *just cause*, and *right intention*, all of which must inform a society's collective decision to engage in armed self-defense. These principles apply to contemporary situations, such as the self-defense of Rwandan Tutsis and Bosniak Muslims in 1994 or the people of Ukraine in 2022.

Saying No: Civil Disobedience, Rebellion, and Revolution

The use of force is traditionally reserved for legitimate public authorities acting within the rule of law. But what about situations when the government is behaving unjustly?

Christians have long repudiated the idea that individuals may self-authorize the use of hateful, unrestrained violence for their own purposes or against governing authority. However, there are other types of actions and cases to be considered. We will first look at some of the differences between political action, civil disobedience, collective self-defense, rebellion, and revolution. The cases of Martin Luther King Jr. and the American colonists in the lead-up to 1776 illustrate key points and crucial distinctions.

In a republican system like those in most Western countries, there are many ways for citizens to seek change or demonstrate their displeasure with existing government policies. Citizens can vote, write letters, support political campaigns, organize like-minded people, set up nonprofit organizations and political parties, engage their elected officials, and run for office. Many Western societies enjoy the fruits of earlier generations establishing the rule of law and high levels of freedom and equality.

At the opposite end of the spectrum is *revolution*, which in effect means the overthrow or destruction of an old system and the forcible establishment of an entirely new system of government. Two examples that epitomize the concept of *revolution* are the French and Russian Revolutions. The French Revolution (1789–99) devastated the country with its guillotine executions of public officials and the systematic destruction of all existing institutions of authority: the monarchy, the nobility, the church, and the lower estates. It was lawless, chaotic mob violence, and most of the revolution's leaders themselves died as a result. In the Russian Revolution of 1917, Lenin and his Bolshevik Communists seized power through societal upheaval and violence, again upending not only the monarchy but all of society's institutions, including religious ones. Private property, free enterprise and the very concept of ownership, church buildings and infrastructure, schools—all were demolished or absorbed by the Communist Party. The Russian Revolution and the subsequent "Great Terror" were responsible for the deaths of anywhere from nine million to thirty million people.

Revolutions typically follow a standard blueprint. First, a small cadre of elites seize power, even if they are carried to victory on the shoulders of an uprising of the masses. Then, that elite imposes its utopian ideology on the country by smashing existing social conventions, laws, and structures and crushing dissent. Typically, much of the populace must be reeducated, and a new dictator emerges to keep the revolution moving forward: Ayatollah Khomeini, Joseph Stalin, Mao Zedong, and Pol Pot are all examples of this type of revolutionary leader. In literature, their tactics resemble the diabolical playbook of "Big Brother" in Orwell's *1984* and of NICE in the third volume of C. S. Lewis's space trilogy, *That Hideous Strength*. Orwell and Lewis were simply modeling their villains on the Russian Revolution and, later, on the rise of Hitler and Germany's National Socialists.

History records a number of other recent examples. For instance, after the Chinese Communists violently seized power in 1949, they came to realize that many existing societal structures created alternative sources of authority and free thinking. Their solution was the so-called Cultural Revolution and the Great Leap Forward. These were really the enacting of their radical ideological agenda, which began with abolishing businesses, libraries, schools, markets, and houses of worship and placing opponents in concentration camps. Over the next two decades the Communists killed or starved an estimated twenty to sixty million people. Cambodia's "Killing Fields" in the 1970s evolved into a similar revolution, designed to take the country back to "Year Zero" and build a utopian Marxist agrarian society by erasing the upper and middle classes and religion through the brutal tactics of Khmer Rouge. This resulted in the planned, callous elimination of nearly a quarter of the population.

The American War for Independence was a far different kind of conflict. That is why many decry calling it the "American Revolution," because it was not a society-upending revolution like those described above. In the case of America, the colonists demanded their rights as Englishmen, not the destruction of private property, elected legislatures, jury trial, and other features of the British common law system. They never sought the destruction of the societal norms and institutions, including the free press, private property, and churches. Later we will look at the decisions that led the colonists to take up arms in self-defense. But first, this chapter will discuss Americans who faced violence for breaking unjust laws to seek peaceful change in a democratic society.

Martin Luther King Jr. on Civil Disobedience

On April 16, 1963, Reverend Martin Luther King Jr. was detained in Birmingham, Alabama. King had been involved in civil rights since the Montgomery bus boycott of 1955 and served as president of the Southern Christian Leadership Conference from its founding in 1957. King knew firsthand just how dangerous it was to advocate for equal rights for all citizens: he had not just received death threats and jail time, but as early as 1956 his home had been bombed.

In order to challenge Birmingham's draconian Jim Crow environment, King and others led a disciplined, nonviolent protest campaign that included boycotts, marches, and sit-ins. King was quickly arrested and wrote a famous essay that we know today as *Letter from Birmingham Jail*. In his letter, King responds to an open letter signed by white Christian and Jewish religious leaders in Birmingham who suggested that he and other civil rights activists were "outsiders" bringing discord to their fair city. He responds by nodding to John Donne: there is injustice in Birmingham and no man, no community, is an island unto itself. We are a part of the whole. We are the *United* States of America. Injustice in Birmingham is injustice in America.

King goes on to define the four steps of his nonviolent campaign. The campaign begins with the careful collection of facts, which are then presented to civil authorities. Second, every effort should be made at negotiation before confrontation. The third step catches most people off guard: *self-purification*. In his *Letter from Birmingham Jail*, King writes that it is difficult to keep feelings of righteous indignation from turning to vindictive hatred. "A process of self-purification" is needed.[1]

How does one do *self-purification*? King's approach is biblical: "Let a person examine himself" (1 Cor. 11:28). From the just statecraft perspective, King is saying that a just cause is not enough. Right intentions are necessary. As King says, civil rights activists had to ensure that they could "accept the blows without retaliating." They met, usually in churches, and talked through what was going to happen. They prayed and sang hymns, and civil rights leaders admonished them to vigilant, loving action. King's *Letter* stresses neighbor-love as the basis for righteous indignation. Righteous anger, whether the anger of Jesus driving illicit money changers from the temple or of bystanders who witnessed the murder of Emmett Till, can be motivated by love. King calls them "extremists for love" and labels Jesus, Paul, Martin Luther, John Bunyan, and Abraham Lincoln as "creative extremists."[2]

King admonished his movement not to fall into hate. Hatred is evil. Hatred is destructive. Hatred, as King well understood, is counterproductive to justice.[3]

King's fourth step is *action*, what he labels "nonviolent direct action," such as sit-ins and marches. "Nonviolent direct action seeks to create such a crisis . . . that a community which has constantly refused to negotiate is forced to confront the issue." He concludes this section, "We have not made a single gain . . . without determined . . . nonviolent pressure."[4]

King always spoke out against retaliatory vengeance and lawlessness. Why? Because lawlessness leads to anarchy. If the goal of a protest event is for *all* people to have *equal rights* and *equal protection* under the *law*, then burning, breaking, vandalism, or looting can never be equated with the nonviolent direct action that King advocates. He goes on, "Nonviolence demands that the means we use must be as pure as the ends we seek. So I have tried to make it clear that it is wrong to use immoral means to attain moral ends. But now I must affirm that it is just as wrong, or even more, to use moral means to preserve immoral ends."[5]

Yet King recognizes that his nonviolent direct action often was a form of lawbreaking. This lawbreaking took one of two forms—either breaking an unjust law or breaking a just law that was being unjustly applied. "Jim Crow laws" that made it impossible for black Southerners to participate in elections were unjust laws. At the same time, many mundane laws, such as the requirement to apply to city hall to receive permits for marches and large-scale events, were implemented in unjust ways to bar black Americans from exercising their First Amendment rights. Whites could hold a parade. Blacks could not. Whites could gather in a public place like a park, but black Americans could not. These laws were enforced, notoriously, by the officers of the law in a way that mocked the blindness of justice.

King bases his argument upon Augustine's declaration that "an unjust law is no law at all." In a moving passage on natural law, King asserts,

How does one determine whether a law is just or unjust? A just law is a man-made code that squares with the moral law or the law of

God. An unjust law is a code that is out of harmony with the moral law. To put it in the terms of St. Thomas Aquinas: An unjust law is a human law that is not rooted in eternal law and natural law. . . . All segregation statutes are unjust because segregation distorts the soul. . . . It gives the segregator a false sense of superiority and the segregated a false sense of inferiority. . . . Thus it is that I can urge men to obey the 1954 decision of the Supreme Court, for it is morally right; and I can urge them to disobey segregation ordinances, for they are morally wrong.[6]

King concludes, "One who breaks an unjust law must do it openly, lovingly . . . and with a willingness to accept the penalty. I submit that an individual who breaks a law that conscience tells him is unjust, and willingly accepts the penalty . . . is in reality expressing the very highest respect for the law."[7]

King was an unsatisfactory prophet to some. As he said in his Birmingham letter, some white "moderates" wanted him to wait until the "right time,"[8] but King knew that without action, justice would never come. He dissatisfied those he called "black nationalists," such as Malcolm X and the Black Panthers, by being too slow, too reasonable, and too forgiving.

Yet King was the prophet who united an unwieldy movement *against* injustice and *for* justice. His *Letter from Birmingham Jail* made common-good arguments that freedom and justice should be the lived experience for all citizens, regardless of race or class. He put the struggle of his day in the context of biblical figures such as Shadrach, Meshach, and Abednego as well as others from history such as the Boston Tea Party's patriots in the lead-up to the American War for Independence and Hungary's freedom fighters against communism (1956).

In conclusion, King's movement did use a type of "force" to shut down businesses and challenge unjust legal regimes. In a sense, people were harmed through lost wages and business on both sides of the divide. Theologian Reinhold Niebuhr observes that Gandhi's marches and boycotts were similarly forceful because they shut down factories and businesses, harming the economy and forcing children to go to bed hungry at night. Both examples, Gandhi and King, were facing representative governments that had rich traditions of civil rights and civil liberties, at least for some. The force of injustice, tyranny by the majority, had to be countered with a countervailing force on behalf of justice. People cooperated, motivated by a just cause, disciplined by right motives. What they were seeking was equality for all under the law, to be protected by government authorities without regard to race or class. This is not revolution and it is not terrorism. King's courageous example and his nonviolent action model provide a framework for evaluating the moral foundation of protest movements in our own time. King was firmly opposed to criminally destructive behavior, such as attacks on citizens, churches, government buildings, and private businesses. Too often vengeful criminality takes advantage of legitimate civil disobedience.

King hoped that "the dark clouds of racial prejudice will soon pass away, and the deep fog of misunderstanding will be lifted from our fear-drenched communities."[9] His persistent, hope-driven efforts catalyzed a national change in America.

Dietrich Bonhoeffer versus Terrorism

When we're looking back on the Nazi decade, roughly 1933–45, it is easy to focus on how many Germans enthusiastically fell in line with the Nazis' aggressive political ideology and demonically racist policies. But there were also Christians who tried to stand up against the Nazis in various ways. Theologian Martin Niemöller was a decorated World War I U-boat commander who, as a German patriot, initially saw much good in the early National Socialist (Nazi) movement. But Niemöller ultimately stood against the Nazis and spent seven years in prison and concentration camps for his stance. After the war he led a theological movement demanding that Germans publicly admit their collective guilt for Nazism and the Holocaust, coauthoring the controversial *Stuttgart Declaration of Guilt by the Protestant Church of Germany* (1945).

Another example is the Austrian Roman Catholic martyr Franz Jägerstätter. Jägerstätter was a small-town farmer of modest means. He was also a patriotic Austrian who served as his local town's mayor and went through compulsory military training. He opposed the Anschluss—the forced integration of independent Austria into the Third Reich—and repeatedly refused to take the required oath to Hitler. As the Tom Cruise film *Valkyrie* depicts, the oath was no small matter. All German and Austrian troops were required to swear a personal oath to the Führer:

> I swear to God this holy oath
> that I shall render unconditional obedience
> to the Leader of the German Reich and people,
> Adolf Hitler, supreme commander of the armed forces,
> and that as a brave soldier I shall at all times be prepared
> to give my life for this oath.[10]

Because he was a farmer, and thus was in an essential profession, Jägerstätter was able to defer military service in the early years of World War II. However, when he was called to active service in 1943, he continued refusing to swear the sacrilegious oath to Hitler. Despite volunteering to serve as a medic or in some other capacity so that he would not participate in killing on behalf of Hitler and the Nazis, Jägerstätter was imprisoned. On August 9, 1943, he was executed via the guillotine.

Perhaps the most famous example is the Protestant theologian and pastor Dietrich Bonhoeffer. Bonhoeffer was one of the pastors who refused to serve in the national German Protestant Church as it came increasingly under the thumb of the Nazis. One of the notorious Nazi policies was to ban individuals of Jewish ethnic heritage, even if they were longtime professing Christians, from participating in local churches. This was one of the many ways that ethnic Jews were marginalized and cast out of society. As early as 1920, the Nazi

Party Platform associated all Jews with the secular materialism of revolutionary communism, as in this party statement: "We demand the freedom of all religious confessions in the state, insofar as they do not jeopardize the state's existence or conflict with the manners and moral sentiments of the Germanic race. The Party as such upholds the point of view of a positive Christianity without tying itself confessionally to any one confession. It combats the Jewish-materialistic spirit at home and abroad and is convinced that a permanent recovery of our people can only be achieved from within on the basis of the common good before individual good."[11]

Bonhoeffer and others actively spoke out against the Nazis and published a statement in 1934 known as the Barmen Declaration. The declaration opposed elevating the Führer as spiritual leader of the church, banishing non-Aryan Christians from ministry, and other perversions of biblical Christianity by a Nazi-affirming religion. Bonhoeffer and his allies set up a rival denomination called the Confessing Church, and for some time Bonhoeffer led a secret seminary to train pastors. Over the next few years Bonhoeffer was increasingly muzzled by German authorities for his anti-Nazi stance. He knew that he could not swear an oath to the Nazis if conscripted, and he sought ways to alert his contacts in the United States, Great Britain, and elsewhere as to just how bad conditions were in Germany. In 1939, he presciently wrote, "Christians in Germany will face the terrible alternative of either willing the defeat of their nation in order that Christian civilization may survive, or willing the victory of their nation and thereby destroying civilization."[12]

As early as February 1938 Bonhoeffer met with members of the resistance who sought a way to end Hitler's rule. Bonhoeffer's intermediary was his brother-in-law, Hans von Dohnányi, who helped Bonhoeffer join the Abwehr, the German military intelligence service. Bonhoeffer kept a low profile within the Abwehr, traveling to nearby countries under its auspices in order to secretly meet with foreign governments and raise the issue of Allied recognition for a German government should Hitler be deposed. Thus, Bonhoeffer directly supported conspirators who sought to assassinate Hitler. On April 5, 1943, Bonhoeffer was arrested, and he spent the next two years in prison. He was ultimately hanged on April 9, 1945, at the Flossenbürg concentration camp, along with six resistance leaders including Admiral Wilhelm Canaris (head of the Abwehr), General Hans Oster, General Karl Sack, and General Friedrich von Rabenau.

Bonhoeffer felt compelled to act in the time of crisis, writing, "If we want to be Christians, we must have some share in Christ's large-heartedness by acting with responsibility and in freedom when the hour of danger comes. . . . Mere waiting and looking on is not Christian behavior."[13] What are we to make of a German pastor and theologian, the author of *The Cost of Discipleship*, going beyond passive resistance to joining an assassination plot and seeking the overthrow of his country's government? Is there a moral basis for this? Was Bonhoeffer a martyr or a terrorist?

Before we look at the larger political issues at hand, it is noteworthy that the Nazi evil hit quite close to home for Bonhoeffer. Bonhoeffer's twin sister, Sabine, had married an ethnically Jewish man. He had many friends who were imprisoned, exiled, ruined, or murdered by the Nazis. Bonhoeffer covertly traveled to communicate with American, British, and other contacts about what was happening to Germany's Jews. When he took an academic appointment in America in 1939, he almost immediately felt duty-bound to cut his time short and speedily return to Germany, even though that move essentially sealed his fate.

Bonhoeffer was a Christian first and foremost, and thus he well understood that he was a citizen in two polities but that his ultimate allegiance must first and always be to the city that has God as its king. Moreover, Bonhoeffer knew that the kingdoms of this earth were measured against the neighbor-love and justice of the city of God, and, therefore, that the Third Reich was opposed to Christ. He made a series of choices that distanced him from the racial dogma and political tyranny of the Nazis, including rejection of what became the blasphemous German national church. He loved his neighbors.

He wanted the best for the German people, and for the human race more generally, and came to believe that what was best in the long run was the defeat of his country's grotesquely evil government in order to stop the sins of Nazism. Bonhoeffer was willing to put his life on the line in order to support that effort, never resorting to criminal acts against civilians or other evil activities that would have directly harmed those outside the Nazi apparatus. He sought, to use biblical terms, the "welfare of the city," not just in Berlin but globally (see Jer. 29:7). Most importantly, as we can see from his voluminous letters and other writings, this was a man motivated by love of God and love of neighbor, not hatred.

Was Bonhoeffer a terrorist? Certainly not. Nor were others who resisted such as Martin Niemöller and Franz Jägerstätter. Rather, they were unlikely heroes and martyrs. Far different are the purportedly Christian liberationist groups such as Joseph Kony's Lord's Resistance Army (LRA) in Africa or the Colombian terrorist organization called the National Liberation Army (*Ejército de Liberación Nacional*, or ELN).

Terrorism is the use of violence by nongovernment actors—usually against noncombatants and private property but also against government targets—that is designed to terrorize the public and change government policy. Terrorists usually claim to be so oppressed that the ballot box is not open to them; however, in reality, terrorists from Che Guevara to Osama bin Laden lack the credibility and support base to win elections, and thus they turn to unlawful violence.

Terrorism, therefore, is not just perpetrated outside rightful political authority; it is a direct assault upon it, just as in the case of Arthur's Black Knight. The Bible teaches that political order is a moral good. Terrorism undermines that order, limiting the reach of the rule of law and eroding public trust. In our time, terrorism often takes on the trappings of "holy war." Terrorism is not just unlawful. It is evil.

One need not go further in the just war criteria than the fundamental tenet of legitimate authority when considering terrorism as immoral and unlawful. However, terrorism fails the other criteria as well. There is no just cause that can legitimize bombing malls, subways, and public buses. It is impossible to conceive of an ethical right intention that deliberately targets houses of worship, grocery stores, and queues in front of public offices. There is no need to go further through the *jus ad bellum* (ethics of going to war) criteria.

Some might object, "Aren't the oppressed sometimes forced to terrorism?" It is important to note that terrorism fails both the basic criteria for going to war and the ethics of how war is fought. Terrorism is a tactic employed by criminals and usually directed at civilians crowded in noncombat zones such as schools, houses of worship, tourist crowds, shopping malls, and public transportation. Therefore, the answer to the question is, simply, "No." It is not true that the terrorist, who deliberately targets the vulnerable in order to spread terror, is just a freedom fighter. Indeed, over the centuries customary international law has come to distinguish legitimate freedom fighters from terrorists. Legitimate freedom fighters, even if poor insurgents, abide by the laws of armed conflict because they represent and seek the good of the local population. They make explicit, public political demands that are for the common good, not merely a revolutionary, religious, or ethnic few. Legitimate freedom fighters may not have expensive, standardized uniforms, but they do wear a patch or insignia demonstrating their identity as members of a combatant organization. They subject themselves to authority within this organization. In just war terms, freedom fighters accept at least two forms of authority.[14] First, they acknowledge customary international law as it is now codified in the Geneva Conventions; second, they submit to some form of organized authority, which means they "are under the command of a person responsible for his subordinates."[15] All of these points are now part of international law, recognizing legitimate freedom fighters in places such as Burma, Kurdistan, Bosnia, and some countries in Africa.

Individuals such as Dietrich Bonhoeffer used unconventional tactics against a superior foe without attempting to terrorize the general populace. We can, therefore, tell the difference between legitimate acts of resistance and ugly terrorism. At one end of the spectrum, the Irish Republican Army deliberately planted bombs in public places, murdering unarmed civilians. They even attacked the British prime minister's residence, 10 Downing Street, with mortars, killing several people. This is terrorism. At the other end of the spectrum, during the 2022 Russia-Ukraine conflict, "weak" Ukraine refused to countenance reprisal (terrorist) attacks on Russian cities. Similarly, General George Washington provides a historical case in point. General Washington operated under civilian political authority, the Continental Congress. He enforced discipline and trained his unprofessional troops. He forbade and punished theft, rape, and abuse of civilians. The Continental Army may have been many things, but it was clearly not terroristic.

You may not have heard of them, but there do exist terrorist groups that claim a Christian justification for their murderous violence. Colombia's ELN justifies its behavior using revolutionary, so-called Christian liberation theology, which is rooted in Marxist dogma. For much of its existence the intellectual vanguard of the ELN was composed of left-wing Roman Catholic priests, most famously Father Camilo Torres Restrepo, a former university professor, who provided much of the weak theological rationale for the movement in its early years. Torres was killed fighting in 1966, but his memory has inspired a generation of radicalized priests and subsequent ELN leaders, such as Spanish priest Father Manuel Perez, who have claimed that Jesus Christ was a revolutionary fighting against oppression and that therefore other revolutionaries have a moral obligation to follow Jesus's example: not simply to be witnesses against corruption in Colombia and in the institutional church but to take up arms until all of Colombia is liberated from injustice, inequality, and poverty.[16] In reality, the ELN employs tactics such as kidnapping, terrorism, and violence against private citizens. It finances itself through demanding ransom for kidnapped prisoners, through extortion for ostensibly "protecting" oil pipelines, and most recently through narcotics sales. A large-scale attack on a public square in 2019 killed nearly two dozen innocent people, wounding over sixty others. The ELN is a terrorist organization that uses lofty rhetoric to justify heinous acts. The ELN's barbarism is more akin to an ideological holy war—where the ends justify *any* means—than to a social justice movement.

In sum, terrorism is morally illegitimate. Terrorism, as an operational strategy, typically attacks "soft" targets such as civilian population centers. Terrorists actively wreak havoc on unprotected civilians, private property, and unsecured government locations. Furthermore, terrorists typically seek haven by hiding within the civilian population. By doing so, they not only violate the principles of ethical combat but also, wittingly or unwittingly, draw civilians into the battlespace. When civilians are killed because terrorists hide among them, using the innocent as human shields, the moral responsibility for those deaths resides, at least in large part, on the terrorist.

Getting Clear about "Holy War"

Militarism, Unrestricted Religious Warfare, and Jihad

Sometimes just war thinking is maligned as being a rationale for *holy war* (jihad, crusade) or *militarism*. For our purposes, *militarism* is the idea that war has its own morality and that military leaders are justified in doing whatever is necessary to win. There are no limits and no political ideologies, only victory or defeat. In the late nineteenth and early twentieth centuries the Prussian (German) high command operated from this view (*Kriegsraison*), and this is what justified the criminal behavior of the German military in World War I, such as unrestricted submarine warfare against civilian ships; what historians call the "rape of Belgium," which included the willful destruction of twenty-five thousand buildings, the murder of civilians, and the displacement of 1.5 million people in the first months of the war; and use of poisonous gases, such as mustard gas. For the militarist, civilians, prisoners of war, and the wounded have no rights. It should go without saying that militarism is not the same as restrained just war statecraft.

This takes us to the waging of unrestricted warfare that has been legitimized by religious justifications. What I have in mind here is not the claim that there is something "holy" or "sacred" involved in a given war, but the overall *sacralizing of all motives and all violence by one side against its enemies*. It is the latter claim that defines "holy war," which more appropriately could be called "religious war," "religion-influenced war," or "religion-inspired war."

Just war statecraft provides us with the framework for critical analysis of so-called holy war. Does a religiously justified conflict observe the criteria of authority, just cause, and right intentions? No. What inspires the individual holy warrior? For some, material gain stimulates participation, as it did for many during the creation of Spain's empire in the New World or for many ISIS (Islamic State) fighters. These were criminals taking advantage of the situation to loot and plunder. Nevertheless, to be fair, at least some holy warriors are motivated by other concerns. For example, some are provoked to action by righteous indignation. Their strongest personal convictions have not only been questioned but affronted and defiled. Some feel compelled to action in defense of those ideals held most dear, the autonomy or even survival of a religious dogma, community, or site. Also, some actively seek an eternal reward. This does not necessarily indicate a death wish, but rather that the individual is convinced that their actions are in pursuit of transcendent ends and that such behavior will please the deity they worship. Of course, some holy warriors seek glory in both the here and hereafter as in the mystical legends of their faith.

In no way do I intend to glamorize or excuse the jihadist or zealot, but I am trying to ensure that we have a window into the sort of tireless and even courageous persistence that has marked some of the fighters we have seen in recent years. For example, the dogged Afghan Taliban, which blends a religious ideology with a localized Pashtun nationalism, seems like a genuine representation of Indigenous religion-inspired fighters, regardless of whether or not we find their views to be despicable. In contrast, terrorists such as the so-called

Islamic State are the worst demonstration of the religious warfare worldview: they seek to purify the land by genocide. Similarly, ideological "holy warriors" like some of Hitler's death squads or suicidal anarchists live in equally perverse ideational universes where religious, cultural, or ethnic differences justify the extinction of "the Other."

Here is the bottom line. Holy warriors will never be content with a peace settlement because they are attempting to inaugurate their idea of God's kingdom on earth. What is even more disturbing is that if the *end* is absolute—the defense of God's name or the religious community or the ideology's dogma—then it is difficult to provide any ethical rationale for limiting the *means* employed. The gloves are off. Anything goes. Hence, the violent excesses of "holy wars": slavery, torture, sterilization, the extermination of entire cities, the quasi-religious philosophy of the kamikaze, and the fatwas of Osama bin Laden resulting in al Qaeda's attacks on civilian populations. For the holy warrior, the end justifies any means. Outsiders—or "Others"— are by their very existence, at least in a given space, unholy and unworthy. Thus, the regular rules and protections of common decency and the law of armed conflict do not apply to them.

In practice, religious wars are usually a downward cycle of violence among ethno-religious groups. They derive their name from religious justifications for extreme violence, often made by those claiming some form of religious authority. It is noteworthy that those quasi-religious authorities are usually not the senior-most authorities in their faith tradition. Osama bin Laden was a private citizen. He had no government or ecclesiastical authority to issue fatwas (religious edicts) calling for the destruction of "the Crusaders and Zionists." Notably, bin Laden also called for the overthrow of the Saudi Arabian government and war on Iran as well.

Thus, in a terrible downward spiral of destruction, "holy wars" usually involve religious people reacting to some provocation. They then justify violence *by their own community* directed at all the members of *a targeted community* (including women and children, the vanguard of the next generation of the "Other" outsiders).

Nonmilitary "soft" targets are often attacked, and when this includes houses of worship—a new, diabolical dimension to the conflict is introduced because believers feel that the sacred has been defiled. Now the cycle evolves into a tit-for-tat, back-and-forth warfare as the violence becomes more and more destructive. Sadly, most wars that follow this path dehumanize the enemy and justify mass bloodshed as a glorious obligation to prove oneself by defending the faith. We have seen the "holy war" mantle used to justify violence between Hindus and Muslims across the Indian subcontinent for the past thirty years.

We also saw elements of this in the Balkans Wars of the 1990s. What began as the disintegration of the multiethnic, federated, formerly Communist country of Yugoslavia turned into a nightmare of atrocities. As the violence spread, led by non- and antireligious political leaders and their criminal henchmen (all former Communists), religious leaders increasingly became involved by giving nationalistic sermons, justifying the arming of citizens, and appearing at militaristic rallies. Some were reacting to the destruction of their churches and mosques by their enemies. One chilling example is the widely available photos of Serbian war rallies showing the "three-fingered salute," associated in Orthodox Christianity with the Trinity, held aloft by crowds chanting for the destruction of their Muslim neighbors. Over time, houses of worship were deliberately demolished, and the violence descended into scenes reminiscent of the Holocaust, where one side tried to exterminate the other. That is so-called holy war in the modern era. It is typically not rooted in disputes over theology, faith practice, or orthodoxy. It is sectarian strife between ethno-religious communities, and, consequently, it is an abomination, whether practiced by "Orthodox" Serbs or by ISIS and al Qaeda.

Christian Theologians on the Books of Deuteronomy, Joshua, and Judges

No major Christian theologian of recent centuries justifies religious violence of the sort we are discussing. Nonetheless, there is another important question for Christians. What do Christian theologians have to say about what appears to be war commanded by God in the Old Testament books of Deuteronomy, Joshua, and Judges? Biblically orthodox theologians over the past two millennia have consistently come to the same conclusion—from Augustine to Calvin and Luther to today's scholars such as Paul Copan. Theologians wisely distinguish between God's commands to his people Israel in the taking of the promised land and other uses of force. The former is a unique case in redemptive history; there is no New Testament analogue. In the case of Old Testament Israel, an omnipotent and loving God had commanded all peoples to honor him, and in case after case humanity refused to do so. God, in his sovereignty, commanded that justice be rendered upon various Canaanite peoples for their idolatrous immorality, and he divinely appointed the Israelites to employ that justice. Note that in the Pentateuch and elsewhere God sets a time when the "iniquity of the Amorites" would reach its zenith (Gen. 15:16). Israel's attack on the Amorites—the peoples of Canaan—was, therefore, not a holy war like those we have seen in the Balkans or the Middle East. This warfare was directly, divinely commanded by God and confined to a specific time and place. It was limited: Israel was not to employ force outside of specific geographical borders, nor was Israel to use it as a means of global conversion by force (there was a mechanism for voluntary conversion in Hebraic law). Israel was not rendering a verdict; God had done so directly, and his commandment was that Israel conquer the land and mete out God's judgment in a way that also returned Abraham's descendants to their homeland. Christians believe that an omnipotent, good God is just in making such determinations but that this is a unique case in history that does not go beyond the explicit command King Saul received to destroy the Amalekites. From David onward, no such commands were given by God to his people. Nor were they repeated in the New Testament. That is because, under the new covenant that continues to this day, God's kingdom expands spiritually and not by acquisition of territory.

Consequently, most Christians look skeptically on the papal claims that drove the Crusades to seek the liberation of Palestine. Christians believe that if a religious figure operates outside of God's explicit divine command and Scripture to enjoin a war of conquest on behalf of religious ends, such action simply does not comport with biblical teaching, whether condoned by a pope in the eleventh century or a Colombian priest in the twentieth century. It is noteworthy that such calls to "holy war" are rooted first in the individual's clerical authority, second in the claim that "holy war" will purify the warrior through struggle and sacrifice, and third in the claim that war will purify the land by cleansing it of unbelievers. Consequently, we would do better to call the Crusades "religious wars" because an ecclesiastical official justified them, but that does not make them "holy," "righteous," or "just." Biblically orthodox Christians believe that it is only through the atoning work of Christ that humanity can be purified, not through individual works or forced conversions.

The American War for Independence

Revolution or Self-Defense? Pastor Mayhew's Sermon

To this point we have looked at a number of the moral issues in contemporary security politics, with a particular focus on resistance. They all involve the use of force and claims of justice. The American civil rights movement and similar efforts, from Gandhi in India to Archbishop Desmond Tutu's coalition in apartheid-era South Africa, used a form of nonviolent direct action that was forceful but not violent. Some people mistakenly think that such an approach is possible in the midst of a violent civil war or international conflagration, but it is beyond credulity to think that peaceful sit-ins, marches, and bus boycotts would have swayed Stalin, Mao, Hitler, or the perpetrators of the Rwandan genocide. Self-defense is morally appropriate; indeed, protection of the innocent is a moral imperative. At the same time, lawless terrorism and unrestrained warfare are never justified. Revolutionary violence that is designed to burn down existing law, institutions, and social norms, such as the French, Russian, and Chinese Revolutions, never meets the definition of a just war.

For Americans, in particular, this brings up a very important question. Was the so-called American Revolution a just war? More specifically, was it just for the colonists to employ force? Based on our categories, it would be better to call the 1776 conflict the American War for Independence because it was clearly *not* a revolution; it was a self-defensive war. After 150 years in North America, the colonists had to make a choice in the 1770s about whether or not they would continue to allow their fundamental rights as British citizens to be trampled upon. Imagine what it would have been like to have been a merchant in Boston or New York in the 1770s, with revenues drying up due to rising taxes and embargoes, not to mention British troops and Hessian mercenaries taking over your home and stables for their own use, with little or no financial compensation, sleeping under your roof not far from your teenage daughter.

Because many citizens in Britain's North American colonies were highly religious, the arguments made by pastors in sermons, both spoken and printed, carried tremendous weight. Pastors such as Jonathan Mayhew, John Tucker, and Samuel West looked to biblical passages such as Romans 13 as well as the works of Calvin, Knox, Ponet, and others, from which they concluded that citizens had a dual obligation to resist tyranny in extreme situations, yet, as much as possible, live dutifully as obedient subjects.[17] A typical example of this is Samuel West's claim that "the same principles which oblige us to submit to government do equally oblige us to resist tyranny."[18] The question is, When does the balance tip to resistance?

The paragon of such sermons is Jonathan Mayhew's 1750 *Discourse concerning Unlimited Submission and Non-Resistance to Higher Authorities*. John Adams, who later served as US president, said that "everyone in the colonies" read Mayhew's famous sermon on colonial rights and that Mayhew was a "transcendental genius . . .

who threw all the weight of his great fame into the scale of the country and maintained it there with zeal and ardor till his death."[19] This
sermon was printed and reprinted numerous times in the colonies
and in London. Mayhew begins with Paul's teaching in Romans 13,

> Let us now trace the apostle's reasoning in favor of submission to the
> *higher powers*, a little more particularly and exactly. For by this it will
> appear, on one hand, how good and conclusive it is, for submission
> to those rulers who exercise their power in a proper manner: And, on
> the other, how weak and trifling and unconnected it is, if it be sup-
> posed to be meant by the apostle to show the obligation and duty of
> obedience to tyrannical, oppressive rulers in common with others of
> a different character.[20]

Mayhew distinguishes between the moral duty of the Christian to
submit to lawful authority and the citizen's appropriate response to
"lawless, unreasonable" tyranny:

> Those who resist a reasonable and just authority, which is agreeable
> to the will of God, do really resist the will of God himself; and will,
> therefore, be punished by him. But how does this prove, that those
> who resist a lawless, unreasonable power, which is contrary to the will
> of God, do therein resist the will and ordinance of God?[21]

Consequently, Mayhew argues,

> Upon a careful review of the apostle's reasoning in this passage, it ap-
> pears that his arguments to enforce submission, are of such a nature,
> as to conclude only in favor of submission to *such rulers as he himself
> describes*; i.e., such as rule for the good of society, which is the only
> end of their institution. Common tyrants, and public oppressors, are
> not entitled to obedience from their subjects, by virtue of anything
> here laid down by the inspired apostle.[22]

This lays the groundwork for action against "tyrants, and public
oppressors." Mayhew's argument goes on at length, articulating a ra-

tionale that increasingly became a part of the colonial consciousness: the purpose of government is to secure the common good. Citizens, working with established political authorities at the local and state level, have a moral duty to resist tyranny.

In sum, it was a member of the black-robed regiment, America's clergy, who provided one of the earliest and most sophisticated theological rationales for the American War for Independence. Mayhew provided this argument in 1750, long before the conclusion of the French and Indian War (1763) resulted in massive taxes on the colonists (e.g., the Stamp Act), before the Boston Massacre (1770) and the Boston Tea Party (1773), and before the redcoats attacked Lexington and Concord (1775). His ideas were directly influential on others, including the framers of a dozen declarations sent to London over the next twenty years.

"The Shot Heard round the World" and the Declaration of the United Colonies (1775)

Violence in North America came to a head in April 1775 in what Americans call "the shot heard round the world." Earlier in the same year, Boston was occupied by British troops who imposed martial law. Although the locals were told they could leave, they were under constant scrutiny and routinely searched. General Carleton, the governor of Canada, was accused of instigating brigands and American Indians to attack frontier settlements. British troops attacked American colonists on April 19, 1775, near Lexington and Concord, and then one day later, on April 20, 1775, Virginia Governor Lord Dunmore ordered the clandestine emptying of the Williamsburg arsenal, a move that was countered by Virginia militia led by Patrick Henry. Subsequent jockeying between the colonials and British troops culminated in the Battle of Great Bridge, near Norfolk, Virginia, later the same year.

After the April 19, 1775, killing of colonists as well as the ongoing British heavy-handedness throughout the colonies, the Continental

Congress laid out its complaints about the violence in July 1775 with the *Declaration of the United Colonies on the Causes and Necessities of Taking Up Arms*. The document provides a rationale for self-defense that completely aligns with just war thinking. The date is noteworthy: it is twelve months, to the week, *before* the more famous July 4, 1776, Declaration of Independence. In the 1775 declaration the colonists beseeched London to not provoke "the calamities of civil war."[23] There is no talk of independence. A careful look at the text of the document shows that it brings together elements from chapter 3 on intermediate authority's responsibility for security and the wider set of just war criteria.

The 1775 declaration begins with a question about legitimate authority: Does God grant to government "unbounded authority . . . never rightfully resistible, however severe and oppressive," or is it "instituted to promote the welfare of mankind"? This is a critical question because it hearkens to the very foundations of just war statecraft, most notably Romans 13:4: "For he [the government official] is God's servant for your good." Because of this, temporal authorities have the responsibility to "bear the sword" to "execute wrath upon him that doeth evil." The colonists were deeply embedded in a Christian worldview, regardless of the unorthodox faith of some prominent individuals such as Thomas Jefferson and Benjamin Franklin. They took Romans 13 and Old Testament examples of moral leadership very seriously, applying them to other founding documents such as the Mayflower Compact and provincial constitutions. Their argument was simple: Political authority is a divinely ordained good. Thus, when political leaders become tyrants, and when there are alternative forms of political authority that will preserve the lives, livelihoods, and way of life of citizens, then it is perfectly acceptable to act in self-defense.

The Continental Congress asked, "What is the purpose of political order in the first place?" This was a question that had been hotly debated in Great Britain over the previous century, as King James and others had argued for a divine right of kings that gave government a carte blanche based on its supreme authority. By the late eighteenth century, some members of the British legislature were making a similar claim: Parliament could do as it pleased. The 1775 declaration by the colonists makes this point: "By one statute it is declared, that parliament can '*of right make laws to bind us in all cases whatsoever . . .*' What is to defend us against so enormous, so unlimited a power? . . . We saw the misery to which such despotism would reduce us."[24]

The colonists argued that London lost its moral authority to govern when it violated its basic responsibility to protect the well-being of citizens within the commonwealth. This includes a variety of threats to their security, both passive and active.[25]

The 1775 declaration argues that governing charters, constitutional rights, and colonial legislatures represent a richer understanding of the political arrangement providing political order in the colonies: "Our forefathers . . . left their native land, to seek on these shores a residence for civil and religious freedom." The writers note that at little cost to the crown, over a period of nearly 150 years, British colonists had, through their own blood, sweat, and fortunes, settled the "distant and unhospitable wilds of America." They were largely self-governing with royal charters; the relationship was so "mutual[ly] beneficial" as to "excite astonishment."[26]

The 1775 declaration transitions from a discussion of legitimate authority to one of just cause:

Parliament . . . in the course of eleven years . . . [have]

- undertaken to give and grant our money without our consent, though we have ever exercised an exclusive right to dispose of our own property;
- statutes have been passed for extending the jurisdiction of courts of admiralty and vice-admiralty beyond their ancient limits;
- for depriving us of the accustomed and inestimable privilege of trial by jury, in cases affecting both life and property;
- for suspending the legislature of one of the colonies;
- for interdicting all commerce to the capital of another;

- and for altering fundamentally the form of government established by charter, and secured by acts of its own legislature solemnly confirmed by the crown;
- for exempting the "murderers" of colonists from legal trial, and in effect, from punishment;
- for erecting in a neighboring province, acquired by the joint arms of Great-Britain and America, a despotism dangerous to our very existence;
- and for quartering soldiers upon the colonists in time of profound peace.
- It has also been resolved in parliament, that colonists charged with committing certain offences, shall be transported to England to be tried.[27]

This is a damning list of trampled liberties. Running throughout it all is a series of taxes ("Acts") that have been imposed upon the colonies one after the other for the previous eleven years, many with the explicit purpose not only of raising revenue but of demonstrating the political primacy of the British Empire. These taxes were buttressed by a naval blockade and various anti-smuggling initiatives designed to choke American trade, and thus threatened the livelihood of thousands of colonists. This was a direct assault on the notions of individual liberty and private property.

The 1775 declaration describes the motivation for this economic warfare: "These devoted colonies were judged to be in such a state, as to present victories without bloodshed, and all the easy emoluments of statuteable plunder." London could pillage its own people, and they were required to submit. And now, the king and parliament had called the self-defensive actions of the colonists "a rebellion" and promised to take "measures to enforce due obedience."[28]

A second set of just cause arguments revolves around the legal rights of citizens within the understood constitutional framework of the British Empire. The colonists were accustomed to trial by jury of their peers, but London had revoked this in numerous instances, setting up an alternative juridical system. Admiralty courts were empowered to deal with many cases, meaning that what had formally been a civil case (e.g., contraband found among legitimate cargo) now could be tried under admiralty law, with no jury nor appeal. Decisions could include the confiscation of the entirety of one's property and imprisonment.

More concerning, however, was that the colonists had every reason to fear being transported to Canada or even London for trial before an inhospitable audience, without recourse to local witnesses and evidence. Additionally, the armies quartered on North American soil, which no longer were focused on fighting the French and which increasingly were in league with American Indians—who at times terrorized the borders of the colonies—all suggested a malign plot to force the colonies into servitude.

In short, the colonists made a classic legitimate authority proposition: London had neglected its responsibilities to them as citizens, choosing a tyrannical course of action to gravely limit the basic rights of the colonists. The colonists also made a just cause argument: their actions were legitimate self-defense. They went on to emphasize their right intention. Their purpose was not to plunder their neighbors or establish a new kingdom.

> Lest this declaration should disquiet the minds of our friends and fellow subjects in any part of the empire, we assure them that we mean not to dissolve that union which has so long and so happily subsisted between us. . . . We have not raised armies with ambitious designs of separating from Great-Britain and establishing independent states. We fight not for glory or for conquest. . . . In our own native land, in defense of the freedom that is our birthright . . . for the protection of our property . . . against violence actually offered, we have taken up arms.[29]

The colonists counted the cost, and they reminded London that there would be a strong likelihood of success if the colonies were forced to defend themselves. Despite the powerful British Navy, the colonists could turn internally for all of the basic resources of life. The North American continent was rich in resources and space, and the colonies had a robust population. The colonies spread over a wide geography that would be difficult for London to tame, particularly if the colonists could achieve some sort of alliance with foreign powers. Such an alliance would not be surprising and would have been seen as clearly threatening by Great Britain: there is little doubt that France, Spain, and others could become involved in a global war like the Seven Years' War (French and Indian War). Furthermore, if some in London believed that they could split off rebellious Massachusetts from "loyal" New York or the southern colonies, the signers of this 1775 declaration insisted on the unity of the colonies. The 1775 declaration concludes with a summary of the strategic milieu: "Our cause is just. Our union is perfect. Our internal resources are great, and, if necessary, foreign assistance is undoubtedly attainable. We gratefully acknowledge, as signal instances of the Divine favor towards us, that his Providence would not permit us to be called into this severe controversy, until we were grown up to our present strength, had been previously exercised in warlike operation, and possessed of the means of defending ourselves."[30]

In conclusion, the colonists reminded London of their many previous petitions, making claims about last resort and proportionality of ends. For a decade, since 1765, individual colonies had sent various petitions and appeals to London, nearly all of which were met with hostility. American representatives, such as Benjamin Franklin, crossed the Atlantic to make their case, but were typically not given audience in official settings. Colonials saw their freedoms reduced, their options limited, and their livelihoods challenged. More specifically, the recent 1774 Coercive ("Intolerable") Acts were essentially acts of war: Boston Harbor was closed, the Charter of Massachusetts revoked, the Administration of Justice Act remitted criminal cases to be tried in Britain, the Quartering Act required colonial residents to house British troops and German mercenaries in their own homes, and the territory of Canada was extended to deny colonists access to Western lands. What was next, the imposition of English bishops? Banishment of dissenters? Mercenary troops sent to conquer the civilian populace? The 1775 declaration finally asserts, "We are reduced to the alternative of choosing an unconditional submission to tyranny . . . or resistance by force. . . . We have counted the cost of this contest and find nothing so dreadful as voluntary slavery."[31]

The American War for Independence was a long and painful ordeal, as every war is. Our history books and Hollywood have helped create images that humanize the issues, the valor, the sacrifice, and the loss of those eight years of war (April 1775–September 1783). It was a war fought, at least on the American side, at first as a self-defensive war buttressed with a moral sense that the colonists' rights, as British citizens, were being trampled and denied or taken away completely. Those liberties, enshrined in the 1776 Declaration of Independence and, later, in the US Constitution and its Bill of Rights, gave a broader moral appeal to the gritty years of war.

When it comes to how the war was fought, Hollywood has taken a bit of the luster off that distant war by showing some of the historical excesses (Mel Gibson's *The Patriot*, A&E's *Turn*) and tragedies of the conflict. We can be thankful that the final peace settlement, however limited, provided a decent start for the new republic. There were no mass reprisals against Tories. There was no postwar dictatorship (as is common after wars of independence). There was no disintegration of political order. The basic objective of 1775—to live in a society based on the English constitutional system of ordered liberty—was realized. Of course, the early American situation had many dangers, whether on the frontier, in the South (Spanish and French territories), in the ongoing British naval and army presence that resulted in the War of 1812, or in the republic falling apart due to intercolonial strife.

The first generations of US citizens muddled along, establishing a secure order, mechanisms for justice, national conciliation among the bickering colonies, and, eventually, a sort of reconciliation with their former British enemies. The American War for Independence was not a "revolution" per se, but it was an important historical moment because it established an amazingly peaceful and prosperous new country. Part of what made that possible was the moral and intellectual leadership of key figures during the War for Independence, most notably George Washington and his lieutenants. They refused to countenance total war directed at civilians, and they treated the enemy with the utmost respect. Indeed, Washington carefully trained and policed his own troops, executing swift punishment if they violated the law of armed conflict. It is to the shaping of those individual warriors that we now turn. What is a moral warrior? How does society nurture a fighting ethos restrained by law and by compassion? The answers to these questions are found in loving the right things in the pursuit of justice.

5

The Motivations and Characteristics of Just Warriors

The Role of Love, Anger, and Virtue

The Germans got us, and they got us right smart. . . . The machine guns were spitting fire and cutting us down," recalled Corporal Alvin York. York's platoon of Americans was ordered out of the trenches in the early morning hours of October 8, 1918, near Chatel-Chehery, France. Corporal York and his comrades were faced with machine guns from an elevated position on Hill 223, just thirty yards away. Only York and a few other privates survived the initial onslaught. "You never heard such a clatter and racket in all your life," York recalled.

German machine guns "mowed down" his comrades, leaving York effectively alone in the field. At this point, a German lieutenant and seven soldiers rushed down the slope at York. "I had my automatic out by then and let them have it. . . . At that distance I couldn't miss."

Miraculously, York was unharmed after the shoot-out with eight
Germans. He then called on the remaining Germans to surrender.
"All the time I kept yelling at them to come down. I didn't want to
kill any more than I had to. But it was they or I. And I was giving
them the best I had."

The rest of the Germans surrendered. The official report said,
"Practically unassisted, he captured 132 Germans (three of whom
were officers), took about thirty-five machine guns, and killed no less
than twenty-five of the enemy, later found by others on the scene of
York's extraordinary exploit." He was quickly promoted to sergeant.
York gave God the glory for saving his life.

York was an unlikely hero. Raised in the backwoods of Tennes-
see, he was one of eleven children in a family that just barely got
by. As a teen and a young man, York was active in church but also
given to drunkenness and fighting. He was twenty-eight years old
when America entered World War I. York was convinced that his
Christian faith in the Church of Christ tradition forbade him to
fight in war.

With this in mind, he filed an affidavit as a conscientious objector,
but it was denied by the US government, and he was sent to boot
camp in Georgia. While there, he trained vigorously but remained
concerned about the moral implications of killing in war. This led
to a series of thoughtful conversations with two of his commanding
officers. This back and forth, rooted in key biblical passages about
justice and responsibility, forced York to reconsider his position. His
commander approved a ten-day leave prior to deployment, during
which York prayerfully grappled with the issues. He returned from
home content that he had a role to play in this war. He later reflected,
"I knew I had to go to France. But I went back to my company trusting
in God and asking Him to keep me, although I had many trials and
much hardship and temptation, but then the Lord would bless me and
I almost felt sure of coming back home, for the Lord was with me."[1]

York could not have known that his expert marksmanship, honed
on hunting to provide food for his struggling family, would save his

life and those of countless others. Perhaps the mixture of his maturity and his deepening faith prepared him to face death on October 8, 1918. His love of neighbor, even his German enemy-neighbor, compelled him to try to save lives whenever possible, even in the midst of the battle.

York earned the military's highest award, the Medal of Honor, for his valor. The citation called his actions a "heroic feat."

What made York a hero? What made his stand in the face of danger heroic? This chapter shifts away from the intellectual frameworks that guide and restrain national security leaders. Now we turn our attention to warriors in the field and what motivates them as they perform valiant deeds in the most trying of circumstances. True, most warriors are not called to undertake death-defying exploits like York. But we want all warriors to have the capacity for heroism, and, thus, we should be concerned with the moral heart and character traits of the just warrior.

To be clear, this chapter is not about physical conditioning, technical training, or raw power, but rather the moral qualities that make a just warrior. Because so many of us immediately think of fictional heroes, from King Arthur to the Marvel pantheon of superheroes, it is important that we ask ourselves, What makes the heart of a hero? Or, better, what characterizes the heart of the just warrior? We will begin by looking at the ways that our history and fiction define the moral attributes of heroes, antiheroes, and villains as a way to orient ourselves to three aspects of the just warrior: *what a warrior loves*, *what makes a warrior angry*, and the *character of the just warrior*. When it comes to character, the four ancient cardinal virtues of prudence, justice, temperance, and fortitude provide a foundation for thinking about the type of warrior that we respect and want to emulate, from the historical Sergeant York to the fictional Captain America. If we want tomorrow's military leaders, and today's battlefield soldiers, to make decisions and act within the frameworks elaborated earlier in this book, then our society must carefully cultivate the ethos of the just warrior.

Differentiating Heroes from Villains and Antiheroes

What is a hero? A hero is someone who fights *against* something larger than himself *for* something larger than himself. Sergeant York was a hero. Sergeant York is representative of our military heroes who risk their lives, or give their lives, to advance the mission and save others. The young shepherd and future king of Israel, David, epitomizes heroism. He stands morally outraged by the blasphemous insults of pagan Goliath, who mocks the living God. Because no one else steps forward, David does. He does not go down to meet Goliath seeking his own glory but rather because "this uncircumcised Philistine . . . has defied the armies of the living God" (1 Sam. 17:36). The Bible is full of examples of those who rise to the occasion during crises: Deborah, Ehud, Gideon, and Abram, who armed his household to pursue the enemy and rescue Lot. Historical figures such as the Continental Army at Valley Forge and the defenders of the Alamo, as well as fictional figures such as the Pevensie children in Narnia, are heroes as well.

Because heroism is the struggle for something larger than oneself against the odds, we often use the term "heroic" or "heroism" for people facing injustice or evil or danger even far from the battlefield. Heroism is about moral choices and moral action. Political leaders may be heroic in standing firm during national crises, as Winston Churchill, Margaret Thatcher, and Abraham Lincoln did. Martin Luther King Jr. was heroic in confronting the overwhelming power of institutionalized prejudice, while facing personal danger and adversity as his home was bombed numerous times and he was unjustly imprisoned. Corrie ten Boom's family and all the others who hid Jews from the Nazis were heroic. Mother Teresa served the poor as a humble nun. For more than a half century she inspired a movement of more than 4,500 nuns committed to caring for "the hungry, the naked, the homeless, the crippled, the blind, the leprous, all those people who feel unwanted, unloved, uncared for, thrown away by society."[2]

The single parent working two jobs, the cancer survivor, the veteran amputee returning to civilian life, the advocate fighting against the odds on behalf of the vulnerable demonstrate heroism as well. Heroism is about the moral quality of the action, not the amount of power at one's disposal.

Hollywood often helps us focus attention on the moral life of those with power, whether they are heroes, villains, or antiheroes. Hollywood's villains use the power at their disposal to deliberately harm others, such as the Wicked Witch of the West in *The Wizard of Oz* or Superman's nemesis Lex Luther. Heroes, in contrast, understand that with their power comes responsibility. Some fictional heroes have extraordinary powers, "superpowers," such as Wonder Woman and Spiderman. Others exercise power inherent in their position or office, such as *Star Trek*'s Captain James T. Kirk with his mighty *USS Enterprise*. Heroes make the moral choice to use the resources at their disposal on behalf of the common good.

Hollywood also portrays a third type, the *antihero*. This is the individual who has power but does not consistently direct his or her will toward or against the common good, but rather wields power selfishly. The antihero acts on self-interest or on the whim of the moment. That whim might appear to be compassionate or vindictive, protective or destructive. This is where the just war principles of just cause and right intention become apparent. Consider the difference between the typical John Wayne Western hero, who protects and defends the weak from predatory criminals, and Wayne's drunken Rooster Cogburn in *True Grit*. Antiheroes on the screen include Tony Soprano, Clint Eastwood's "man with no name," Deadpool, Captain Jack Sparrow, Marvel's Black Adam and Loki, and many others. The antihero may act as the good guy in one situation but be the villain in the next. The antihero has power but shuns responsibility. He is untrustworthy, self-seeking, and intemperate.

The antihero is relevant here because we cannot assume that power and justice necessarily go together without right intentions. In practice, our military and law enforcement focus a great deal on physical fitness and technical preparation. There is no guarantee that this will result in soldiers having the moral compass and inner fortitude to do the right thing, particularly when the chips are down. One never knows when heroism will be called for until it is. Alvin York was unexpectedly called to it one October morning in 1918. The teenage shepherd David was delivering supplies to his elder brothers when the giant Goliath taunted the Israelites in the Valley of Elah. David stepped up. A hero is often made by being in the right place—or rather, what might seem like *the wrong place*—at the right time. That is when moral decisions are made.

Not everyone will be called to be heroic, but every one of our guardians should absorb the moral resources to be a just warrior. Developing the just warrior first includes nurturing the right motivations, including an appropriate love of country, love for their comrades, and love even for their enemies. We must cultivate these qualities in all of our young citizens and, especially, those who volunteer to serve as our protectors, guardians, and warriors.

Nurturing Right Motivations

Love of Country

I joined the US military as an Air Force reservist at the end of 1996, and I witnessed many young people volunteer to serve in the aftermath of the September 11, 2001, attacks. What compelled them to volunteer? What I typically heard among those volunteering to serve was, "We were attacked," and therefore "I felt that I had to do something." But they did not say this with a spirit of blind vengeance. They said it with righteous indignation inspiring a desire to protect and defend.

A friend of mine who was a young music educator at the time was one of those volunteers. He was never going to be a Navy SEAL, but he signed up. At first he was assigned to be a chaplain's assistant, an enlisted role to help and protect chaplains. Later his musical talents were put to use in a military band as a part of the National Guard. In that role, he provided humanitarian relief in the aftermath of several hurricanes on the Gulf Coast, was activated for COVID-19 duty for four months, and served on the US-Mexico border. He was part of an Air Force musical group that entertained US and coalition troops in Iraq and several other Middle Eastern countries. He volunteered. His country put him to work.

Similarly, former NFL star Pat Tillman left a lucrative career with the Arizona Cardinals to fight terrorism. He and his brother, Kevin, enlisted in the wake of 9/11. Tillman earned a place with the Army Rangers, fought in Iraq, and tragically died by friendly fire in the dangerous wilds of Afghanistan. Tillman said that his service was a no-brainer: "Somewhere inside, we hear a voice. It leads us in the direction of the person we wish to become. But it is up to us whether or not to follow."[3] Like Tillman and my friend the musician, many voluntarily protect the rest of us by responding to their nation's call with whatever talents they possess or develop through training.

What is this love of country that makes a person feel that he or she must "do something"? In *The Four Loves*, C. S. Lewis provides an answer. Lewis describes several ways we can think about love of country. At the bedrock of this is *love of home*.[4] Home means all that is familiar, from familiar faces to familiar places. Home is the sense that I am part of a community. I share life and experiences with my neighbors and kin. Such love of our immediate neighbor helps us recognize that our primary obligations are, first and foremost, to those closest to us. God put us in a specific time and place to reflect him and serve others. We simply cannot exercise the same degree of neighbor-love to everyone, everywhere, all of the time. To do so would be to neglect those for whom we are responsible at home. At the same time, our love of neighbor should, according to Lewis, elevate our view of our fellow human beings as bearing the image of God. It should help us lift our eyes away from narrow parochialism to lovingly see God's design in all of humanity.

Lewis argues that we have expanding circles of what is shared, and part of this is our common national story.[5] This is a building block of patriotism. That story helps us to understand where we came from and how we got here. It is a narrative that looks at our history with a sense of thanksgiving but also with an eye of critical discernment. We should be inspired by what is noble and special in our nation's history and ideals while striving to overcome our nation's shortcomings.

Love of home and love of country should not be culturally chauvinistic. Lewis says that we should recognize that just as it is right for me to love my home with its idiosyncrasies, so we should naturally expect a Frenchman to love and be proud of his home and the Japanese to love and be proud of their homeland.[6] Rightful patriotism includes respect for difference.

Appropriate love of one's homeland differentiates proper patriotism from inappropriate or even violent forms of nationalism. The term "nationalism" has shifted in meaning in recent years. It used to mean the simple idea that the cultural identity of a people is or should be tied to a specific geographical place, such as the Kurds in Kurdistan or Koreans in Korea. But when nationalism goes beyond that simple idea to embrace a chauvinistic ethnic or ideological political program, it is badly misdirected. We see such examples in the violent ethno-religious nationalism of Sri Lanka's Sinhalese leadership, the Burmese government with its ethnic cleansing of the Rohingya minority, or Han China's assault on the Muslim Uighurs. These forms of love-my-clique are sinful because they categorize the "Other" as not simply different but of lesser moral value. This is a gross violation of Christ's command to love one's neighbor.

We can see how the sin of hypernationalism is related to a form of political idolatry. Many extreme social and political "isms" such as communism, fascism, hypernationalism, or ethnocentrisms such as India's violent Hindu nationalism are idolatrous in putting a government, ethno-religious identity, or ruling ideology at the center of meaning and existence. Making a political ideal the centerpiece of a worldview is a theological move, one that displaces God and his transcendent moral order in favor of human power and will for a particular place and time. Hypernationalism whitewashes the sins in a nation's past. This is collective self-adoration, whether expressed at Babel, or in the hubris of Athens and Rome, or in the idolatrous systems of the French and Russian Revolutions. These are wrong *loves*.

It is not surprising, therefore, that in places such as China, North Korea, and elsewhere today, Christians are seen as obstacles for their unwillingness to bow to the maximizing demands of the state. Daniel, Shadrach, Meshach, and Abednego all faced this challenge of allegiances. Christians in Rome faced this when confronted with mandatory emperor worship. Today's Christians in Communist countries face it when restricted from worshiping or when government policy mandates abortions. The Christian may love community and country, but his or her highest allegiance is to something above the political party or the government. A Christian's first allegiance, his or her first love, is devotion and obedience to Jesus Christ. Love of Christ, informed by Holy Scripture and led by the Holy Spirit, must be the essential loyalty and animating motivation for the Christian.

It is not only right but also admirable to appropriately care for the good of the community and nation where God has placed us. Patriotism loves what is good in our own country and respects the patriotism of others. Our nation should never be set up as the ultimate center of truth and authority. That is reserved for God and his Word. The lyrics of "America" ("My Country, 'Tis of Thee") express this affectionate balance well:

> My country, 'tis of thee, sweet land of liberty, of thee I sing.
> Land where my fathers died, land of the Pilgrims' pride,
> From every mountainside let freedom ring!

> My native country, thee, land of the noble free, thy name I
>   love.
> I love thy rocks and rills, thy woods and templed hills;
> My heart with rapture thrills like that above.

Our fathers' God to Thee, Author of Liberty, to Thee we
    sing.
Long may our land be bright, with freedom's holy light,
Protect us by Thy might, Great God our King.[7]

Love of Comrades

Another love characteristic of the just warrior is love of comrades.
One of the things that I learned in the military was that people often
join in order to gain benefits, such as a paying job, travel, and the GI
Bill to fund college. People reenlist to stay in the military, however,
because of their devotion to their country and, especially, their fidelity to their comrades.

We have noble words for this love of comrades: loyalty, faithful-
ness, fidelity, steadfastness, duty, dependability, constancy, and the
like. The US Marine Corps' official motto, set to music by John Philip
Sousa, is *Semper Fidelis* ("Always Faithful"). "Semper Fi" means fidelity to the nation and to one's brothers and sisters in arms. Individuals
in a military unit forge bonds as a team due to what is shared: shared
training, shared mission, shared commitments, shared values, shared
danger. These communal experiences bind individuals into a sort of
family. Indeed, it is hard for many warriors to express the significance
of these bonds to their actual family members.

Think for a moment about the heroes and heroines of the most
popular movie franchises. The heroes almost always are rooted in a
tightly knit group of comrades with whom they share the fight. Villains often deride that loyalty as a weakness, to their own peril. In
the Harry Potter series, Voldemort tells Harry that his friends make
him weak. The goddess Athena tells Percy Jackson, "Your fatal flaw is
personal loyalty" (*The Titan's Curse*). Lord Palpatine says essentially
the same thing to Luke Skywalker in *The Return of the Jedi*. But
Harry, Percy, and Luke each overcome evil as a part of a close circle
of allies. The same is true elsewhere in fiction. Tom Cruise's Ethan
Hunt in *Mission Impossible* refuses to leave a teammate behind. It

takes a company, a band of brothers, to destroy the Ring and save Tolkien's Middle-earth. Black Widow, played by Scarlett Johansson, explicitly calls her allies in Marvel's Avengers "family," as does Vin Diesel's tight-knit crew in the *Fast and Furious* franchise. Such fictional heroes stand ready to make extraordinary sacrifices for their comrades. *Star Trek*'s Spock was willing to give his life to save his comrades: "The needs of the many outweigh . . . the needs of the one."[8] Boromir of Gondor sacrificed himself so that Frodo and his companions could escape to carry on their quest to defeat evil in J. R. R. Tolkien's *Lord of the Rings* trilogy. What could be more heroic than facing death to save others?

The heroic, sacrificial action that these characters take on behalf of their friends reflects the image of biblical love, from Jonathan defying King Saul on behalf of his friend David to Christ's sacrifice on the cross. This is what speaks to our hearts when someone "takes a bullet" to save another. That kind of valor stirs something in us. It inspires us. It makes us want to emulate this devotion. Jesus explained it: "Greater love has no one than this, that someone lay down his life for his friends" (John 15:13).

Fiction is a pale reflection of those who in reality hazard their lives serving in law enforcement, the military, and the intelligence community. Lance Corporal Kyle Carpenter jumped on a grenade in Afghanistan to save his comrades' lives on November 21, 2010. Amazingly, he lived to receive the Medal of Honor. He exemplified selfless sacrifice.

Such love of comrades is a worthy and appropriate love. What is much harder, though, is how to extend Christ's injunction to love one's neighbor when that neighbor seeks our harm. Is it possible for the just warrior to love his or her enemies?

Love of Enemies

On a trip to Iraq in 2010, one of my American colleagues needled our translator, "Why can't you Iraqis just forgive and forget? You used to live side by side as neighbors. Why seven years of bloodshed and needless violence?" The translator, an Iraqi Kurd in his early twenties, replied, "Let me tell you my story." He vividly recalled his father racing into the house screaming, "Flee, flee to the mountains. . . . Go out the back door. . . . Run. . . . Do not stop! The helicopters are coming!" The seven-year-old boy fled to the hills, with his four-year-old sister in tow as Saddam Hussein's Sunni forces invaded their town. It took three days to reunite with his parents. Many friends and relatives were massacred. Much of their community was obliterated.

"You ask me to forgive?" he murmured, almost to himself. Then he said, "I've been educated in the West and have somewhat of an outsider's view. I think I can put it aside, intellectually, and then my children will be able to 'forget.' But my family and neighbors forget? Forgive? I do not think my generation can forgive our enemies and it certainly cannot forget. Maybe our children, or their children."

C. S. Lewis made a similar remark during a wartime radio lecture in 1943: "Forgiveness is a lovely idea . . . until you have something to forgive. . . . I wonder how you'd feel about forgiving the Gestapo if you were a Pole or a Jew?"[9]

If we are going to talk about loving our neighbor, we must deal with the hard case, when our neighbor is our enemy. This brings up all of the moral and spiritual issues attendant to situations of loss, bitterness, and injustice. How, then, should one love one's enemies? To answer that question, Lewis drew the attention of his listeners to the second half of Christ's injunction to love your neighbor *as you love yourself.* Lewis queried, "Well, how exactly do I love myself?"

> Now that I come to think of it, I have not exactly got a feeling of fondness or affection for myself and I do not even always enjoy my own society. So apparently 'Love your neighbor' does not mean 'feel fond of him' or 'find him attractive' . . . [or] thinking them nice either. . . . In my most clear-sighted moments not only do I not think myself a nice man, but I know that I am a very nasty one. I can look at some of the things I have done with horror and loathing. So apparently I am allowed to loathe and hate some of the things my

enemies do. Now that I come to think of it, I remember Christian teachers telling me long ago that I must hate a bad man's actions, but not hate the bad man; or, as they would say hate the sin but not the sinner.[10]

Righteous indignation directed at injustice is appropriate. We will look more at such appropriate anger later in this chapter. Lewis warns against allowing ourselves to be overtaken with bitterness or cynicism. It is easy to fall into the trap of damning our enemy for their beliefs or actions, dehumanizing them. Just as we do not dehumanize ourselves, we must recognize the humanity, the humanness, of our enemies.

But loving one's enemies, or one's friends for that matter, does not rule out *justice* according to Lewis: "Does loving your enemy mean not punishing him? No, for loving myself does not mean that I ought not to subject myself to punishment, even death. If you had committed a murder, the right Christian thing to do would be to give yourself up to the police and be hanged. It is, therefore, in my opinion, perfectly right for a Christian judge to sentence a man to death or a Christian soldier to kill an enemy."[11] Lewis went on to discuss the nexus of justice and right intentions. Neighbor-love, even of our enemies, challenges us to kill—to use Lewis's term—the egotistical part of our *own* nature that feeds on bitterness. "We may kill if necessary, but we must not hate and enjoy hating. We may punish if necessary, but we must not enjoy it. In other words, something inside us, *the feeling of resentment, the feeling that wants to get one's own back, must be simply killed. . . .* That is what is meant in the Bible by loving him: wishing his good, not feeling fond of him nor saying he is nice when he is not."[12] Lewis's argument presupposes the principles of just war statecraft that I have been discussing in this book, with a particular focus on the state of our hearts. Times of injustice and violence are likely to provoke anger. Right intention means being on guard against unjust anger and hatred, and this is crucial for the just warrior.

Anger, Hatred, and Love

Christians over the centuries have asked questions about anger in the context of conflict, fighting, and war. Is anger a sin? Is anger the opposite of love? Aren't Christians called to love, not to anger? These questions are crucial when we think about the heart of the just warrior.

Scripture makes important distinctions concerning anger. Ephesians 4:26 admonishes: "Be angry and do not sin." Theologians have long distinguished hatred from righteous indignation. Christ's example of anger against money lenders in the temple and against the hypocritical religious leadership of his day shows us that anger is not sinful in every instance.

As a result, we need to distinguish two main categories of what causes us to become angry. The first category involves those things that affront the ego: *my* pride, *my* status, *my* rights. We experience this temptation every day: "How dare they speak about me that way . . . cut me off in traffic . . . not give me my due . . . ?" Bruised egos ready to flare up at any moment result in anger that is sinful because it is rooted in self-centered pride. This is why the Bible warns us to be "slow to anger" (Prov. 15:18). In Matthew 5:21–24, when Jesus warns against stoking sin in our hearts, he particularly highlights hatred, which he equates with murder and adultery.

There are a variety of ways that self-centeredness leads to unjust anger. The *Star Wars* epic gives us an example in Anakin Skywalker, a gifted young man who becomes the evil Darth Vader. Recall what Jedi Master Yoda says to a young Anakin at the Jedi Council in *The Phantom Menace*: "Fear leads to anger. Anger leads to hatred. Hatred leads to suffering."[13] Anger is not hatred, but fanning the flames of one's anger into wrath will lead to obsessive, destructive, hateful behavior. Yoda recognizes that there are things that motivate anger that are not based in love. In Anakin's case, he experienced injustice as a child causing fear and resentment, which spawns hatred that he stokes until he becomes a mass murderer and the most feared dark knight in the galaxy.

In stark contrast to hateful anger is loving anger. This species of anger has to do with injuries to the rights and fundamental dignity of others. It is entirely appropriate to feel and express righteous indignation rooted in love of neighbor and love for justice when confronted by the sins and tragedies of this world.

The *Star Wars* series presents us with another young Jedi warrior who is motivated by righteous indignation: Luke Skywalker. When he is barely more than a teen, his aunt and uncle are slaughtered by the Empire's storm troopers. However, Luke does not give in to vengeful hatred. Later, Luke and his father (Anakin, who became Darth Vader) are brought before the evil Emperor Palpatine. This is a moment of truth. Luke has every right to be vengeful: He was raised an orphan because his father joined the Dark Side. He was lied to about his parentage. His adoptive relatives were massacred. He was powerless in all of this, but now he is a trained, though young, Jedi warrior. History seems to be replaying itself.

In a moment when Luke is despairing that his friends and his cause are lost, Emperor Palpatine tries to tempt Luke to turn against his father and destroy him. This is the same way Palpatine tempted Luke's father decades before: "I can feel your anger. It makes you stronger. . . . Let the hate flow through you." Refusing to be pulled into the moral trap of harming his father, Luke vows, "I will not turn" to the Dark Side. Luke refuses to be lured into acting based on hate: he feels righteous anger about the loss of family and friends, his father's terrible choices, and the wickedness of Palpatine, but he will not kill vengefully. Instead, he turns to his father, Darth Vader, pleading, "Father, let go of your hate!" Luke tries to rescue Vader. Luke sacrificially sets down his light saber rather than commit hate-driven violence against his father at the evil emperor's urging.

Luke and Anakin both experience strong feelings of anger, but one anger is righteous indignation focused on justice and protection, whereas the other is murderous and prideful.

Imagine, if Yoda had expressed the trajectory of loving anger, perhaps to Padmé or to Luke: "Love leads to anger. Anger inspires self-sacrifice and justice. Justice lays the foundation for peace." Martin Luther King Jr., Dietrich Bonhoeffer, or Mother Teresa could have uttered these sentiments, because they lived by them.

Righteous indignation, then, should be about much more than someone stepping on my toes. Loving anger is outrage motivated by love: love of neighbor, love of country, love of justice, love for a type of world we all want to live in. Certainly, my own basic human rights may be a part of realizing such a world, but they are connected to the same rights of others. Moreover, anytime we think in terms of rights, we also need to be thinking in terms of responsibilities. As Christians, we particularly need to consider our responsibilities to our fellow human beings, who are made in the image of God. Righteous indignation is rooted in our common humanity and our responsibility to defend, protect, and serve others made in the likeness and image of God. This begins with those closest to us, our families and neighbors, and expands from there. Philippians 2:4 talks about this when it says, "Let each of you look not only to his own interests, but also to the interests of others."

Lewis says that appropriate righteous indignation is a sign of moral health because of its direct tie to justice. In his *Reflections on the Psalms* Lewis worries about vapid citizens who lack a moral center: "Thus, the absence of anger, especially that sort of anger which we call indignation, can, in my opinion, be a most alarming symptom. And the presence of indignation may be a good one."[14] Lewis goes on to say that those who lack appropriate righteous anger when confronted by injustice may have "no conception of good and evil whatsoever."[15]

Lewis similarly ties righteous anger to the concept of justice. He reminds us that the Bible is full of calls for justice, particularly in the Psalms and the Prophets. Looking at such passages in the Psalms, he observes, "We find they [the authors] are usually angry not simply because these things have been done to them, but because these things are manifestly wrong, are hateful to God as well as to the victim."[16] Righteous anger and the desire for justice recognize that God's creation, which he created as good, is out of alignment with God's purpose. Lewis concludes that the psalmists' curses remind us of God's holy character and holy anger.

Too often the fight for what is right evolves into hatred of not just the evil done but the evildoers themselves. According to Lewis, God's righteous wrath is directed toward sin, not sinners. This is the example for us to follow. "Against the banality of modern morality, the ferocious parts of the Psalms serve as a reminder that there is in the world such a thing as wickedness and that it (and not its perpetrators) is hateful to God."[17]

To be sure, even our righteous indignation on behalf of a good cause must be limited and routinely checked. Lewis warns that we can allow righteous anger over injustice to boil into vengeful passion. "We must not give our indignation full vent, to sacralize it as holy . . . to add, implicitly or explicitly, 'Thus saith the Lord' to the expression of our own emotions or opinions."[18] We have a biblical example of this in Moses's violent temper. In times of injustice, Moses gives full vent to his wrath, causing himself tremendous suffering. We see multiple instances of Moses's anger. When he is a prince of Egypt, his rage over injustice leads him to murder an Egyptian overseer. At Kadesh (Num. 20), Moses rages at the faithless Israelites, "Must we bring you water out of this rock?" Moses disobeys God's command to speak to the rock and instead ferociously strikes the rock. For this he is denied entry to the promised land. Despite legitimate reasons for just anger, Moses gives his indignation "full vent," which is sin.

This is where "love your enemies" and righteous indignation over injustice intersect. Lewis writes, "Christianity does not want us to reduce by one atom the hatred we feel for cruelty and treachery. We ought to hate them. . . . But it does want us to hate them in the same way in which we hate things in ourselves: being sorry that the man should have done such things, and hoping, if it is anyway possible, that somehow, sometime, somewhere he can be cured and made human again."[19] Lewis has much more to say about the intersection of justice, righteous anger, and bitterness in his works. Appropriate love of country, love of comrades, and a loving recognition that an enemy remains one's neighbor restrains and channels the righteous indignation that the just warrior, and indeed all of us, feel when confronted with injustice. The question before us is, What traits should citizens and defenders develop to ensure that they have the character of just warriors?

Cultivating the Right Characteristics

What are the fundamental characteristics of the just warrior? It is not enough for us to say that senior leaders make decisions and the just warrior must simply follow orders. Being under authority is very important, so we will discuss what that looks like. Yet it is noteworthy that almost all security services articulate virtues that they want their members to exhibit. The US Army, for example, emphasizes seven core values: loyalty, duty, respect, selfless service, honor, integrity, and personal courage. The core values of the other branches of the US armed services, as well as those of our closest allies such as the United Kingdom and Canada, look very similar. Police and other first responders also display core values. When we look at these principles, we find them all in the Bible in some way or another. Moreover, when we look at our historical heroes, such as Sergeant York and George Washington, as well as fictional heroes, such as King Arthur and Aragorn, they embody such principles. Superman's historic ethos embodies this: "Truth, Justice, and the American Way."

We will now look at how just war reasoning shapes our understanding of the moral warrior in two dimensions. First, the just warrior is under the authority of those in command as well as under the moral authority of law. Second, key character traits of the just warrior include the cardinal virtues of prudence, justice, temperance, and fortitude.

The Just Warrior Is under Authority

First and foremost, just warriors are under authority. That authority takes one of two forms, and those forms are usually intertwined. The first is the authority of the *office*. The second is the authority of *law*. The former means that some leaders, by virtue of the office they hold, give the order for the preparation, training, planning, and implementation of the use of force. Legitimate political authorities authorize the use of force. We call this "command authority." In the United States, the Constitution specifies that the power to command the armed forces belongs to the president as commander in chief, but the Congress provides the resources for warfare and has the authority to declare war, not the president. The commander in chief's authority is delegated down to senior civilian and military leaders and down the ranks to officers, sergeants, and those who command operations in the field. The foundational principles of law and justice call on those in command authority to exercise power to protect the vulnerable, punish wrongdoers, establish security, and deter, as much as is possible, unlawful violence and criminality. Those who serve in the military are under this lawful command authority.

The second form of authority is that of law. There is a fundamental moral law—what many call natural law—that expresses itself in centuries of moral codes, legal precedent, the practices of statecraft known as "customary international law," and the formal law of armed conflict. As Christians, we know that the foundation of this is the moral law that God expressed in the Bible and that Jesus summarizes as the outworking of the commands to "love the Lord your God" and to "love your neighbor as yourself" (Matt. 22:37, 39). In the opening of the book of Romans Paul writes about this natural phenomenon of the moral law "written on [the] hearts" of all people (2:15). This natural law is the bedrock for a society to function, and it is why training is so essential. Today's military trains personnel to distinguish legitimate targets from civilians and private property. Training directs them to act in accordance with the rules of engagement so that warriors will act with integrity and humanity in the field. This is all founded on a fundamental belief that there is a difference between right and wrong, which reflects the reality that there is an underlying natural law.

Recognizing that our warriors are under these two intertwined forms of authority is crucial when we think about battlefield violations of what is right. The vast majority of orders that our soldiers receive are lawful, and we expect them to follow those orders willingly and vigorously. But what about the unlawful or immoral order? The most obvious case is the German soldier assigned to immoral duty at a concentration camp during World War II. This is not theoretical: people like Franz Jägerstätter were ordered to take an oath to Hitler and serve him unquestioningly. Most did. The few who did not faced execution as traitors, but how much more horrific for their soul and for their country would it have been if they instead were obedient to the immoral orders of Hitler and the Nazi commanders? The US massacre of villagers at My Lai in March 1968 is another case in point. American soldiers decimated a Vietnamese village, brutally killing civilians and gang raping women and children. It was only stopped when a brave helicopter pilot, Major Hugh Thompson, and his crew directly intervened by blocking US soldiers from getting at their victims and also reported the massacre of civilians. The sadistic platoon leader on the scene, Lieutenant William Calley, claimed to have been merely following orders. He was convicted in 1971 for his part in conducting the massacre.

In general, soldiers should refuse to carry out immoral, unlawful orders even if it exposes them to risk of punishment for disobedience. They must uphold what is right according to the moral law. The reason that we expect them to do so is that they are moral agents and there is a law higher than any political leader, an ultimate morality upon which civic laws and civilization are founded. Senior political and military authorities are supposed to embody that law. When they do not do so and order something that is immoral, the just warrior must carefully decide how to respond and should not obey that which is immoral and unlawful.

The Just Warrior Is Virtuous

The Bible in many different places describes the qualities of the moral person and the moral leader, from the book of Proverbs to the fruit of the Spirit listed in Galatians 5:22–23. We can see these virtues at work in the fundamental character of the just warrior—from Joshua to David's "mighty men" to Sergeant York in World War I to fictional superheroes in literature and movies.

More specifically, theologians and philosophers refer to prudence, justice, temperance, and fortitude as the four cardinal virtues. The term "cardinal" comes from the Latin word for a door hinge, suggesting that these foundational virtues are the hinge upon which other moral characteristics proceed. These virtues are found at various points in the Bible and have been referred to as a group by theologians such as Ambrose and Augustine.

As we have seen, soldiers and sailors are under the command of political authority. That means the primary decisions about strategic just cause and right intention are in the hands of legitimate authorities who then issue orders for action. As a people, we should direct our hope and effort to ensuring that the souls of the people who carry out those orders exemplify prudence, justice, temperance, and fortitude on the battlefield.

The first cardinal virtue is prudence, which is the practical wisdom to contextually understand the times—more specifically, this time and this place—and to respond with wise, appropriate actions. Prudence basically is good judgment. Prudence also recognizes the moral implications of action versus inaction. The prudent warrior uses skill and knowledge in how he or she acts or reacts. The book of Proverbs contains a storehouse of teaching on prudence, such as counting the cost of building a defensive fortification or seeking mature counsel before engaging in war. The principle of stewardship that we discussed in chapter 2 characterizes the prudent warrior. The descriptions we have of Joshua, Caleb, David, and some of David's warriors, such as Joab and Ira the Jairite, portray them as both shrewd tacticians and skillful warriors.

The second cardinal virtue is justice, which involves both fairness and righteousness. Justice-as-fairness begins with the notion that the role of a guardian is to protect citizens and thwart evil. The moral warrior is an agent of justice. Justice-as-righteousness indicates the ethical compass of the just warrior. The just warrior acts from a heart of righteousness, what we used to call "uprightness" or "rectitude." Uriah the Hittite, whom David callously murdered by purposely having Uriah sent to the front lines, where the battle was the fiercest, appears to have been a righteous man. He would not sleep in comfort with his wife while his comrades were at the front. David's lieutenant, Benaiah, who went on to serve Solomon faithfully as a sort of enforcer, was similarly just.

Temperance, or self-control, is the third cardinal virtue. Temperance includes sobriety, restraint, and moderation. The intemperate warrior loses control and causes or wields reckless, indiscriminate violence. The intemperate warrior often indulges himself in the illicit fruits of victory, glorifying violence and pleasure from sex, risk-taking, and wanton destruction. Solomon and Samson are described in the Bible as lacking temperance, and their lack of control over their own desires haunts their legacies. *The Iliad* provides a number of cases in point. Perhaps the most glaring lesson involves the consequences of Achilles's utter lack of restraint as well as his moral pettiness. Homer's tale begins with murderous rage:

> Sing, Goddess, Achilles' rage,
> Black and murderous, that cost the Greeks
> Incalculable pain, pitched countless souls
> Of heroes into Hades' dark,
> And left their bodies to rot as feasts
> For dogs and birds.[20]

The Iliad ends with Achilles's death after his vile desecration of the body of his noble foe, Hector. Achilles was intemperate and sought only to feed his own appetites for glory, sex, and companionship. In contrast, the temperate warrior is mindful of the state of his own heart and exercises restraint in his actions. We see this in York, who fought vigorously yet temperately, keeping a watch on his own heart. He fought toward the goal of peace and avoided hatred, as witnessed by his calls for the German troops to surrender instead of gunning down more of them.

The fourth virtue is fortitude, which is both battlefield bravery and moral courage. The brave warrior faces obstacles, enemies, and fear but chooses to stand up against adversity. Sometimes that is on the battlefield, but it can also be in the murderous realm of politics. In the Bible, Joshua and Caleb demonstrate fortitude in serving as spies, fighting as warriors, and unpopularly challenging the disobedience of the Israelites. Other judges of Israel, including Gideon, Deborah, and many others, courageously face dire odds on the battlefield. Also, a number of prophets such as Jeremiah face death as traitors for giving political advice that the kings in Israel do not want to hear. Hezekiah, the moral king of Israel, courageously stands up to the massive armies of Sennacherib. Shadrach, Meshach, and Abednego could probably have used their high government status to avoid controversy, but publicly face off with Nebuchadnezzar by refusing to bow to his image when ordered to do so. These are all portraits in courage.

Similarly, we love to cheer the worthy underdogs of our fiction who bravely overcome fear with modest resources to fight for what is right, as do Harry Potter, Katniss Everdeen, Tris Prior, and Frodo Baggins. This is the kind of moral impulse we need to nurture in our youth.

But fortitude is not just battlefield bravery; it also means *moral courage*, doing what is right even if it is counter to what is popular or what is expected. The characters noted above all exhibit moral courage. They show mercy when they have the opportunity, and perhaps the right, to kill. They evaluate their motives and the motives of others. They speak up and stand up for justice. They refuse to take advantage of their unique skills, power, or position. They challenge injustice, unjust authority, and immoral power regimes. Through all the struggles, they show an inner strength that serves as a moral compass and a secure foundation upon which they stand. This is fortitude worthy of Paul's admonition in Ephesians 6:13: "Therefore take up the whole armor of God, that you may be able to withstand in the evil day, and having done all, to stand firm."

Conclusion: Training Warriors, Cultivating Virtue, and Avoiding Moral Confusion

How does one develop the cardinal virtues of prudence, justice, temperance, and fortitude? As Marc LiVecche writes in his superb book on moral injury, the first steps begin in the institutions of our society and how we raise our children.[21] The reason this chapter focused some attention on differentiating heroes, antiheroes, and villains is that our society is constantly talking about power and influence, from so-called social media "influencers" to Hollywood superhero movies. Whether we like it or not, we are surrounded by a never-ending discussion about morality, power, and responsibility. It is in our news (e.g., Afghanistan, Russia) and in our entertainment. And if our churches and families are avoiding conversations about moral responsibility in a violent and fallen world, that simply means that our younger citizens are getting an earful, or iPhone-ful, from non-Christian sources.

Our families, churches, and schools need to refocus on raising moral citizens whose consciences are shaped around virtues such as prudence, justice, temperance, and fortitude. It begins with what we talk about, what we read, and what we watch in our homes. We need to transmit to young people the nobility of public service, particularly public service where love of neighbor requires facing danger and self-sacrifice. This is the opposite of glorifying violence for its own sake, such as through violent movies and video games. It is also quite different from a vague Christianity that suggests that love is the absence of criticism. That phony sort of love results in a morality that affirms everything because it doesn't dare be judgmental. This is a source of society's moral confusion.

This moral confusion is detrimental to the spiritual and psychological health of our protectors and guardians. Recall my earlier discussion differentiating lawful force from vengeful violence. If our society's message is that the real-world use of force is necessarily sinful, and at best constitutes a "lesser evil," then we are creating a scapegoat culture within our law enforcement, military, and security communities. We are telling those who protect us that they, by virtue of their calling and work, have "blood on their hands" anytime they arrest a criminal or try to stop a crime that is being committed. A government official in Robert Ludlum's famous *Bourne* series says that secret government agents are the "sin eaters" of society, doing evil so that citizens could live in peace. There is absolutely no biblical justification for this view. The only person who can and did take on the sin of others is Jesus Christ. Our warriors may sacrificially interpose themselves, using force and being the victims of violence, but they do not necessarily have "dirty hands" simply because they wear a uniform or badge.

Such "lesser evil" viewpoints create moral confusion for people, who need instead to learn about the moral use of power to combat injustice. This "lesser evil" idea is wrong and can be damaging to soldiers, who are misled to think they have participated in an evil by engaging in war, rather than having stood for justice in a sinful world. Just warriors, if under proper authority, are acting virtuously when they prevent, punish, and protect, even if it means using lethal force against evildoers. This moral clarity is urgently needed in our public discourse about war and peace.

The cardinal virtues are a good place to start. They serve as a framing lens for thinking about how we train just warriors. They also give guidance about the lessons to draw in teaching our children about models of just warriors, whether at church, at school, in literature, or on screen. We should make a point of highlighting these lessons to our children: the prudence of biblical Joseph as well as Hogwarts' Dumbledore, the just nature of Abraham as well as Aslan, the temperance of Nehemiah and Sir Galahad, and the fortitude of Esther and Mordecai, Reepicheep, the Three Musketeers, and many others.

All of this leads us to the final aspect of Christian just war thinking: the goal of peace. I discussed peace in an earlier chapter, but we have yet to consider how a society is reconstructed after the physical and social destruction of war. Because Christians are called to be agents of healing and reconciliation in our neighborhoods and communities, we should be particularly interested in the ways that postwar environments can take steps toward order, justice, and conciliation.

6

Ending Wars Well

Order, Justice, and Conciliation

In C. S. Lewis's *The Lion, the Witch and the Wardrobe*, Aslan presents the Pevensie children with gifts they are to use in their roles as the kings and queens of Narnia. Peter, as high king, is given a sword and shield. Susan is given a bow and a horn. When that horn sounds the alarm, help will come. Lucy is given a small dagger and a vial of precious healing ointment. One of the most poignant scenes in the Narnia adventures is when Lucy, acting as a sister (private citizen), wants to focus her attention on her wounded brother, Edmund, rather than acting responsibly in her vocation as queen by caring for the crowds of wounded around her.

> They found Edmund . . . covered in blood, his mouth was open, and his face a nasty green color. "Quick, Lucy," said Aslan. And then, almost for the first time, Lucy remembered the precious cordial. . . . Her hands trembled so much that she could hardly undo the stopper, but she managed it in the end and poured a few drops into her brother's mouth.

"There are other people wounded," said Aslan, while she was still looking eagerly into Edmund's pale face and wondering if the cordial would have any result. "Yes, I know," said Lucy crossly. "Wait a minute."

"Daughter of Eve," said Aslan in a graver voice, "others also are on the point of death. Must more people die for Edmund?"[1]

The point is that Lucy, in her role as queen with the gift of a healing potion in her hands, has a responsibility to serve and heal, just as Susan has a responsibility to sound the alarm and Peter has a responsibility to protect and defend. Lewis's fictional account reminds us that God calls and empowers some people to public service vocations, just as the Bible shows examples in the lives of Joseph, Nehemiah, and Cornelius.

Public servants and citizens have a range of callings and stewardship duties related to statecraft and conflict. This chapter focuses on how wars end and the diversity of professions that support peace and justice, from diplomats and humanitarians to warriors to medical professionals and psychologists. In short, Christians have roles to play as agents of peace across all the dimensions of conflict, including the rebuilding of broken political systems, the search for justice—for both victims and aggressors—and efforts at postconflict conciliation.

Ethics at and beyond War's End

Christians are rightly concerned about peace. In chapter 1 we considered the appropriate definition of peace, distinguishing the internal peace of the individual from external and collective forms of peace. At war's end, building an enduring and secure peace is daunting. It requires arriving at some sort of concord between adversarial governments and communities who have been locked in mortal combat. Our framework for the ethics at war's end, what just war statecraft calls *jus post bellum*, involves the three principles of order, justice, and conciliation (see sidebar).

Order, Justice, and Conciliation

- *Order*: Legitimate authority has the capacity to provide basic government services and security from internal or external threats.
- *Justice*: Establishing a just peace may include consideration of individual punishment for those who violated the law of armed conflict and restitution policies for victims when appropriate.
- *Conciliation*: The parties come to terms with the past so that they can imagine and move forward toward a shared future.

A society at peace is a secure, rightly ordered community that is at peace with itself and with its neighbors. This societal peace forms the basis of the "tranquility of order." To achieve such societal peace, postconflict settlements should exhibit restraint in their terms while pursuing justice (restitution, punishment), in contrast to a so-called victor's peace, which is based upon vengeance and destruction. The just war approach to ending conflict is moral in seeking punishment and restoration as well as focusing on a shared, secure future rather than on revenge for historic or imagined grievances. Figure 6.1 demonstrates how a hardy political order can lay the groundwork for efforts to restore justice and, ultimately, achieve conciliation.[2]

Figure 6.1 Ending Wars Well—Building Blocks
Adapted from Eric Patterson, *Ending Wars Well* (New Haven: Yale University Press, 2012).

Order: Governance, Domestic and International Security

Americans, Canadians, Britons, and other Westerners reading this book often take political order for granted. But in many places around the world, domestic political concord, order, cannot be assumed. People in Sudan, Ethiopia, Afghanistan, parts of Central America, and many other countries have not experienced true peace at home. Order means, first and foremost, a basic level of security at home. As we saw in chapter 2, there is a general principle of governance in human groups and institutions, and that is what a society that is coming out of war needs. An orderly peace requires at least three basic conditions: governance, internal security, and security from external threats.

Basic governance, or political order, means that a legitimate government has the ability to provide basic services to the public, such as access to water and sanitation. In postconflict situations, humanitarian aid is typically directed first to these human survival and basic subsistence needs to forestall social collapse, disease, and famine. With the loss of life and injury due to warfare, government has much to do to bind up the physical wounds of the nation.

At the same time, order also means that society is not under violent threat from internal or external enemies. In such a situation, there is little threat to law and order from local terrorists, insurgents, or dissatisfied revolutionaries. Similarly, the populace is not at the mercy of criminal networks, such as Latin America's narco-kings or African warlords. Another dimension of security and regional peace involves the government facing no immediate or existential threat from a neighboring country. Often postconflict societies are weak, their borders are porous, and they are vulnerable to armed groups, criminals, and strong neighbors. True order at war's end means that there is now the potential to build a more secure peace so that governance may take root. This state of peaceful sustainability represents a "tranquility of order."

To Western eyes this is a very modest conception of order. It does not necessarily include guaranteed free education for everyone, ad-

vanced healthcare systems, flourishing universities and public libraries, or many other wonderful services. These are the *fruits* of peace,
not the *roots* of peace. The root of societal flourishing and peace is
basic order sustained over time. People who have traveled to impov-
erished areas in South America or Africa realize that there is a lack
of governance, basic law and order, in these places that leaves them
exposed to a cycle of disorder and injustice.

Justice: From Whom and to Whom

The pyramid structure of figure 6.1 implies two things. The first is
that postwar settlements need to move through order to justice and
that many postconflict situations do not make it to the justice phase.
Putting justice before order does not work. It does not make sense to
try to hold war crimes tribunals while gunfire blazes outside the door.
The second implication is that order and justice should, over time,
be mutually reinforcing and thus create greater stability for a society.

Moral accountability, in its fullest sense, includes both a *from
whom* and a *to whom*. Another way of saying this is that justice
attempts to hold those responsible accountable on behalf of their
victims through *punishment* and *restitution*.

Postconflict justice requires moral accountability for past actions,
including the decisions by leaders that led to war in the first place.
This is where postconflict justice takes into account the just war criteria of who made the decision to go to war and why they did so, the
criteria of authority, just cause, and right intention. There should be
accountability for those in power who are responsible for provoking
conflict. True, the breakdown of international peace is a complex
set of circumstances, but in many cases war is directly attributable
to the aggressive policies of a specific regime or cabal within the
regime, such as Hitler's Nazis or the radical Hutu genocidal attacks
in Rwanda (1994). Leaders are responsible for peace and security,
and when they abrogate that obligation, it may be appropriate to
hold them accountable in postconflict settlements. Often all that is

possible, though, is to defeat them on the battlefield. That is often punishment enough.

The same is true for misdeeds in warfighting. Soldiers and their leaders on both sides are responsible for their conduct during the conflict. A richer notion of a just peace is one in which steps are taken to hold accountable those who willfully broke the laws of war on the battlefield—those soldiers and/or sailors who violated the restraining principles of military necessity, proportionality, and discrimination. One thing that Americans are rightly proud of is the fact that not only do we try to hold others accountable for such crimes, but our military polices the actions of our own troops as well. The world was rightly shocked, for instance, by American misdeeds at My Lai during the Vietnam War and the perverse behavior of US soldiers at Iraq's notorious Abu Ghraib prison. Some of those involved in both of these events were court-martialed by the US military. Such self-scrutiny and accountability are not exercised in the cases of Syrian troops massacring their own people, Chinese officials torturing Uighurs in Xinjiang Province, or Russian military personnel murdering civilians during the 2022 Ukraine invasion.

Punishment, in theory, is punitive action against a wrongdoer, but what does it look like in practice? It may mean loss of rank or position, fines, imprisonment, exile, or death. Punishment is the consequence of the forsaking of responsibility and an important feature of postconflict justice. It makes an abstract conception of accountability concrete by employing sanctions against those responsible for initiating violence or transgressing international law and the rules of warfare. For many reasons, this type of accountability typically must be limited in scope, lest it undermine a fragile order. Wars between governments typically do not result in an unconditional surrender, but rather some sort of modest settlement. Thus, we have to think about how to pursue and implement justice on a case-by-case basis.

The destructive nature of war means that a complete return to the prewar status quo is impossible and may not be desirable in some cases, such as in situations of secession or civil war. Citizens, both in and out of uniform, have died. Vast sums of government-controlled funds have been expended. Natural resources and regions of land have been used up or destroyed. Justice takes the cost of war, particularly the cost in lives and materials, into account and argues that, when possible, aggressors should provide restitution to the victims. This principle applies both to inter- and intrastate conflict: at war's end aggressors should remunerate, when appropriate and possible, the wronged.

Restitution is very hard to accomplish in practice. Consider the case of a classic historical war in Europe prior to 1900 between two governments, often ending in some sort of stasis and then a peace treaty. In other words, the two sides get stuck, write a treaty adjusting some borders here and there, exchange prisoners, and go home. Winners often win a little, losers have historically not lost everything. This sets up a situation of sturdy postconflict order without justice and certainly without conciliation. One side may be forced to pay an indemnity, but the money goes to the government and not as reparations to citizens and communities. These types of arrangements have usually worked to keep warfare fairly limited.

It is easy to see, then, just how daunting it is to implement practical policies of societal restoration. It is easier to seek a limited order and, in some cases, targeted justice against perpetrators rather than to do an accurate accounting and collect the bill from a former adversary. It may be best to find a way to commemorate what was lost, through memorials and public testimony, rather than try to monetize it. This brings us to the practical politics of seeking conciliation.

Conciliation

A Christian approach to postconflict looks toward conciliation, defined as coming to terms with the past, so that we can see our former adversaries as partners in a shared peace. This is not easy. The principles of order and justice provide a foundation for political conciliation among nations who were formerly in conflict. Such conciliation is the ultimate step toward building a durable framework for domestic and international peace. It is noteworthy that political conciliation between governments is usually not based on feelings of affection or idealistic visions of global harmony. Efforts at political conciliation must be rooted in government's responsibility to protect its citizens and secure a just peace and an enduring peace settlement.

Usually it takes a prudential judgment by experienced statesmen about how best to secure peace, and this typically begins with a thoughtful evaluation of the national interest: Is it really in the best interests of our country to experience more of the terrible costs of war? Often political conciliation between former adversaries is nudged along by a reevaluation of common threats. For example, at the end of World War II bitter enemies, France and West Germany, allied together within NATO due to the colossal threat of Soviet Communism. The same was true in the Far East as Japan and the neighbors it had brutalized, led by the United States, created an alliance called SEATO (Southeast Asia Treaty Organization) to contain Communist advances. New alliances among old enemies prevented additional bloodshed. Over time, those alliances of convenience can deepen. By the 1980s it was hard to imagine the French and Germans going to war.

This is not to say that the best peace settlement that one can hope for is merely rooted in shifting alliances. There are cases where Christians or Christianity-inspired principles for seeking justice and conciliation directly lower tensions, overcome injustice, and establish peace. Here are four examples.

The Truth and Reconciliation Commission in South Africa

First, the fact that apartheid-era South Africa did not disintegrate into civil war and later developed its Truth and Reconciliation Commission is largely due to the influence of Christian teaching, expounded and modeled by inspirational religious leaders such as

Anglican archbishop Desmond Tutu, who laid out an alternative to mass violence and retribution. Starting in the early 1980s, Tutu led civil rights marches (in the style of Martin Luther King Jr.) against the apartheid South African regime. In his speeches he famously paraphrased the Bible: "If God be for us in our struggle against injustice and oppression, who can be against us?"

With the end of apartheid in 1993, Tutu, Nelson Mandela, and others believed that societal healing needed to blend justice and forgiveness. South Africa's Truth and Reconciliation Commission realized the need for some form of justice despite a very fragile political situation, and it required admissions of guilt by perpetrators and the public testimony of victims before providing a sort of amnesty to agents of the old regime. Many victims testified that this process brought them a level of healing because their experience was vindicated, even though they did not receive financial compensation and even though many perpetrators received political mercy after admitting guilt. Tutu reflected, "The only way to experience healing and peace is to forgive. Until we forgive, we remain locked in our pain and locked out of the possibility of experiencing healing and freedom, locked out of the possibility of being at peace."[3] Did the commission solve all of South Africa's problems? No, but it did provide a mechanism for political transition and a level of social conciliation seen almost nowhere else in the world. It was up to future leaders to build on this foundation or turn their backs on it.

CHRISTIAN PEACEMAKING IN WAR-TORN MOZAMBIQUE

Unfortunately, most of South Africa's neighbors did experience horrific civil wars as they emerged from colonialism. Mozambique is a case in point. The departure of the Portuguese regime in 1974 created a power vacuum that was occupied by two rival forces, known to the West as RENAMO and FRELIMO. As in most Third World proxy wars of the 1960s to the 1980s, one side received patronage from the anti-Communist West, and the other from the Communist

Soviet bloc. It was an ugly, vengeful war that lasted for more than a decade, with few rules.

Enter a Roman Catholic lay organization called Community Sant'Egidio. The doctors, lawyers, and other professionals of this Italy-based religious organization based their calling on Matthew 9:35–37: "Jesus went through all the towns and villages, teaching in their synagogues, proclaiming the good news of the kingdom and healing every disease and sickness. When he saw the crowds, he had compassion on them, because they were harassed and helpless, like sheep without a shepherd. Then he said to his disciples, 'The harvest is plentiful but the workers are few.'"[4] Representatives of Community Sant'Egidio began visiting war-torn Mozambique armed with medical and humanitarian provisions, which they freely dispensed to people on both sides of the conflict. Planes and shiploads of desperately needed supplies arrived over the next several years. In 1982, the community mediated between the opposing sides, resulting in the release of some priests and nuns who were being held by RENAMO forces. Over time, Community Sant'Egidio volunteers developed deep personal contacts within both RENAMO and FRELIMO and, in 1990, organized secret, informal meetings in Rome between the belligerents under the cover of World Cup matches. Later that year Community Sant'Egidio hosted formal talks at its private offices in Rome. Over time the US and Italian governments and United Nations were pulled into a formal political process. One can see the spirit of reconciliation in an address at an early negotiating session by the community's leader:

> Many serious problems exist in the past and in the future. We are aware that every problem can give rise to misunderstanding and that the interpretations which are made are very different. Will we be able to resolve them . . . ? Let us strive to find that which unites rather than that which divides. The desire for that which unites can also suggest to us a working method, the spirit of this meeting. That which unites is not little, rather there is a great deal. There is the great Mozambican family, with its very ancient history of suffering. . . . The unity of the

Mozambican family has survived this history of suffering. We find ourselves today, if you will allow me to say, before two brothers, truly part of the same family, who have had different experiences in these last years, who have fought each other. . . . Conflicts with outsiders pass; between brothers it always seems more difficult. Nevertheless, brothers will always be brothers, notwithstanding all the painful experiences. This is that which unites, to be Mozambican brothers, part of the same great family.[5]

After eleven meetings over twenty-seven months, a peace deal was reached on October 4, 1992. The final agreement explicitly echoed these sentiments by making reference to "Mozambican brothers." Community Sant'Egidio's peace-seeking friendships and sacrificial giving were indispensable to building the trust necessary for a formal peace settlement.

ABRAHAM LINCOLN AND THE US CIVIL WAR

The demands of the US presidency drove Abraham Lincoln to prayer and daily Bible reading. He routinely cited biblical passages and religious themes, including judgment, punishment, love of neighbor, and reconciliation, such as this from his second inaugural address in 1865: "Fondly do we hope—fervently do we pray—that this mighty scourge of war may speedily pass away. Yet, if God wills that it continue, until all the wealth piled by the bond-man's two hundred and fifty years of unrequited toil shall be sunk, and until every drop of blood drawn with the lash, shall be paid by another drawn with the sword, as was said three thousand years ago, so still it must be said 'the judgments of the Lord, are true and righteous altogether.'"[6] Lincoln called the Civil War a "fiery trial," for him as president and for the country. He encouraged others to look to the ultimate judge: "Let us diligently apply the means, never doubting that a just God, in his own good time, will give us the rightful result." He thanked Christians for praying for him and the war effort: "God bless the Methodist Church—bless all the churches—and blessed be God, Who, in this our great trial, giveth us the churches."[7] Using Scripture, he challenged the entire concept of slavery: "To read in the Bible, as the word of God himself, that 'In the sweat of *thy* face shalt thou eat bread,' [but] to preach from there that, 'In the sweat of *other men's* faces shalt thou eat bread,' to my mind can scarcely be reconciled with honest sincerity."[8]

In looking at war's end, Lincoln kept his eye on moral victory. He wrote, "We accepted this war for an object, a worthy object, and the war will end when that object is attained. Under God, I hope it never will until that time."[9] He saw purpose, even in war.

> The purposes of the Almighty are perfect, and must prevail, though we erring mortals may fail to accurately perceive them in advance. We hoped for a happy termination of this terrible war long before this; but God knows best and has ruled otherwise. We shall yet acknowledge His wisdom and our own error therein. Meanwhile we must work earnestly in the best light He gives us, trusting that so working still conduces to the great ends He ordains. Surely He intends some great good to follow this mighty convulsion, which no mortal could make, and no mortal could stay.[10]

Lincoln was inspired by biblical texts about restoration and reconciliation, as when he referred in his second inaugural address to the need to "bind up the nation's wounds," alluding to Psalm 147:3, which influenced his philosophy for how the Civil War should end. He told a delegation from Pennsylvania that he intended to avoid self-righteous policies, "so that we may not, like Pharisees, set ourselves up to be better than other people." He inspired Congress: "And having thus chosen our course, without guile, and with pure purpose, let us renew our trust in God, and go forward without fear, and with manly hearts."[11]

President Lincoln famously told his foremost generals, Grant and Sherman, that they must "whip" the Confederacy and then, using a wrestling analogy, "let them up easy." He told the Secretary of War that forgiveness toward Confederate troops, not extracting postwar

guilty pleas, was the best posture. Lincoln recommended liberal amnesties so that the Confederate rank-and-file soldiers would be able
to peaceably return home: "On principle I dislike an oath which requires a man to swear he *has* not done wrong. It rejects the Christian
principle of forgiveness on terms of repentance. I think it is enough
if the man does no wrong *hereafter*."[12]

Lincoln was directly opposed by the radical Republicans of his own
party who hungered for postwar vengeance. One of Lincoln's most
strident critics, Pennsylvania senator Thaddeus Stevens, thundered,
"The future condition of the conquered power depends on the will of
the conqueror."[13] Looking back from our vantage point today, would
the US have fallen into civil war or long-term insurgency, as Jefferson
Davis demanded, if such vindictive policies had been implemented?
Fortunately, despite Lincoln's assassination, his vision was carried out
by his successor, Andrew Johnson, who faced impeachment for his
moderate vision of postconflict justice and conciliation. The punishment of the South's devastating battlefield defeats was followed by
three amnesties for Confederates who would swear an oath to the
Union and return home unmolested. Later, general-turned-president
Ulysses S. Grant continued policies of national reconciliation and
unity, however imperfect. Unlike Afghanistan or Congo or Sudan,
or Europe during most of its history, the post-1865 US did not fall
back into civil war.

Woodrow Wilson and the Fourteen Points

Virginia-born president Woodrow Wilson was an important American leader and academic who served as president of Princeton University and governor of New Jersey. Today, Wilson's accomplishments
have come into question because of some of his Southern-formed
attitudes, particularly on race. Nevertheless, Wilson—the son of a
minister and a practicing Presbyterian—routinely cited Scripture and
his faith as the primary influences on his view of statecraft. Facing the
inevitable end of grisly World War I, Wilson introduced his famous

Fourteen Points as a vision for a postwar global order rooted in the Golden Rule. In his January 18, 1918, speech to the US Congress outlining these points, Wilson begins,

> It will be our wish and purpose that *the processes of peace, when they are begun, shall be absolutely open* and that they shall involve and permit henceforth no secret understandings of any kind. *The day of conquest and aggrandizement is gone by*; so is also the day of secret covenants entered into in the interest of particular governments and likely at some unlooked-for moment to upset the peace of the world. It is this happy fact, now clear to the view of every public man whose thoughts do not still linger in an age that is dead and gone, which makes it possible for every nation whose purposes are consistent *with justice and the peace* of the world to avow now or at any other time the objects it has in view.
>
> *We entered this war because violations of right had occurred* which touched us to the quick and made the life of our own people impossible unless they were corrected and the world secure once for all against their recurrence. What we demand in this war, therefore, is nothing peculiar to ourselves. It is that the world be made fit and safe to live in; and particularly that it be made safe for every peace-loving nation which, like our own, wishes to live its own life, determine its own institutions, be assured of justice and fair dealing by the other peoples of the world as against force and selfish aggression. All the peoples of the world are in effect partners in this interest, and for our own part we see very clearly that unless justice be done to others it will not be done to us.[14]

In practice, Wilson believed that the way to overcome the conditions that led to World War I was to recognize the political equality of all people and all nationalities; hence his insistence on national sovereignty for groups within the old Austro-Hungarian Empire, transparent diplomacy without secret treaties, free trade and transparent commerce, and freedom of the seas for all parties in war or peace. We can also see the blend of establishing a new and more equitable order, basic justice for oppressed groups, and a view toward conciliation among governments and peoples. Wilson concludes the speech,

> For such arrangements and covenants we are willing to fight and to continue to fight until they are achieved; but only because we wish the right to prevail and desire a *just and stable peace* such as can be secured only by removing the chief provocations to war, which this program does remove. We have no jealousy of German greatness, and there is nothing in this program that impairs it. We grudge her no achievement or distinction of learning or of pacific enterprise such as have made her record very bright and very enviable. We do not wish to injure her or to block in any way her legitimate influence or power. We do not wish to fight her either with arms or with hostile arrangements of trade if she is willing to associate herself with us and the other peace-loving nations of the world in covenants of justice and law and fair dealing. We wish her only to accept a place of equality among the peoples of the world, the new world in which we now live, instead of a place of mastery.[15]

Although some breezily say that the 1920s–1930s was a failure of international diplomacy because Hitler rose to power in Germany, many people in Europe at the time did not see the Versailles Treaty and Wilson's Fourteen Points as a failure. Poland was dismembered from 1795 onward, but the Second Polish Republic was established in 1918 under Wilson's plan. Romania, Serbia, and Montenegro received their independence, Belgium was restored, Hungary was finally free from Austria, and modern Turkey was guaranteed some level of independence. Germany transitioned to a parliamentary form of government, however unsteadily. Hence, despite its limitations, the post-1918 concord was of great benefit to many societies. Moreover, the next generation of statesmen, led by Winston Churchill, Franklin Delano Roosevelt, and Harry S. Truman, would learn from the failures of appeasement during the 1930s and initiate an even more sweeping postconflict order in 1945–48 that was to better approximate order, justice, and conciliation: the Nuremberg and Tokyo war crimes tribunals, the Marshall Plan providing desperately needed economic assistance to rebuild Europe (it was even offered to the Soviet Union!), the Truman Doctrine to protect democracies, the establishment of NATO to counter the Soviet Union's aggression in Eastern Europe, the global "Bretton Woods" economic system of free and lawful trade, revised laws of armed conflict such as the 1949 Geneva Conventions and Genocide Convention, and the inauguration of the United Nations and the Universal Declaration of Human Rights.

The Morality of Victory

The triumphs of 1865 and 1945 remind us that victory matters. Unfortunately, in some quarters there is a suspicion that fighting to win is somehow unseemly, that striving for victory is something for which to be ashamed. C. S. Lewis wrote that he could not understand the "sort of semipacifism you get nowadays which gives people the idea that though you have to fight, you ought to do it with a long face and as if you were ashamed of it."[16] J. R. R. Tolkien agreed: the victory of Aragorn and the lords of Middle-earth meant a decisively different moral order than the conquest and brutality of Sauron's reign. If we think about victory from the standpoint that the goal of war should be a better state of peace, then industrious, sustained efforts to win are virtuous.

Taking a step back, there are three types of victory in war. The first two are rather obvious. The first type of victory is classic, decisive battlefield victory. Rome defeated Carthage, Caesar beat the Gauls, Napoleon bested the Austrians, and the US-led allies won in 1918 and 1945. Lincoln's United States of America smashed the Confederacy in 1865.

A second form of victory occurs when one side blocks the other side from achieving its aims. This is usually the case of the weaker party outlasting a stronger rival. George Washington and the Continental Army refused to give up and kept the British Empire from winning for over seven years. Ultimately the British Parliament decided it could not win on its terms, and America won its independence. Insurgent armies in Vietnam and Afghanistan have likewise followed the strategy of winning by not losing.

There is a third type of winning that is qualitatively different. I will call it "moral victory." In some, but not all, cases the victor imposes its ethical framework on the loser. If Hitler had won World War II, he would have imposed Nazi "morality" on the vanquished. In fact, he did so for several years in Poland, Germany, Austria, and parts of Czechoslovakia. The Nazis had an evil system based on racial preference, anti-Semitism, and Aryan supremacy. Had they held more of their European conquests, their noxious system would have deepened across Europe. Because the alliance of the United States, Soviet Union, and United Kingdom ultimately won, we saw two different moral systems take root in the spheres of influence of the Soviets and the Americans. In the West, the democratic and capitalist system that privileges human rights and individual freedoms took hold. In the East, the Soviets imposed a Communist "morality" of totalitarian domination and Marxist orthodoxy that tried to eradicate religion in all the countries taken over by the Soviet Union. The Communist Viet Cong and the ruthless Taliban also imposed their "moral" strictures on their subjects.

Winning matters because a new political order will be shaped by those in power at war's end. We desire for wars to end well, to end in accord with the moral framework that brings a just peace. Earlier in this chapter we read a segment of Abraham Lincoln's second inaugural address, given just forty-one days before his assassination. In its entirety, Lincoln's magnificent speech summarizes how the principles of order and justice are wrapped up in the morality of one political system triumphing over another one. He concludes with a vision of conciliation:

> With malice toward none; with charity for all; with firmness in the right, as God gives us to see the right, let us strive on to finish the work we are in, to bind up the nation's wounds; to care for him who

shall have borne the battle, and for his widow, and his orphan—to do all which may achieve and cherish a just, and lasting peace, among ourselves, and with all nations.[17]

Christian Vocations in All Phases of War

The US government has a number of frameworks for thinking about diplomacy, international competition, and the use of force, two of which can help us understand the wide range of potential activity for Christian citizens. The first framework is called "DIME," and it relates to what US foreign policy doctrine labels the "four elements of national power."[18] Every country defends and promotes its interests and ideals through diplomacy, information and intelligence, military power, and economic avenues. This is just as true for Tahiti, Togo, and Trinidad as it is for the US. Diplomacy means all of the ways that a government interacts with other governments, from bilateral meetings between ambassadors to engagement at the United Nations. The US has been particularly strong since World War II in leading the way, via diplomacy rather than force, toward norms of democracy, human rights, and collective security among the old enemies of Europe and Asia. Part of this success is where formal diplomacy meets information, including the "soft power" of America's democratic and economic success, which most people around the world desire to replicate. Information, as an element of national power, covers everything from the attractiveness of American ideals, such as those stated in the Declaration of Independence, to US media freedom to cybersecurity. Of course, another obvious element of national power is economic success, which the US has enjoyed in unparalleled fashion for much of the past century and which can be deployed to assist the poor through USAID's humanitarian assistance or applied to sanctioning nefarious actors including Russian oligarchs, criminal cartels, and terrorist networks. America's military power is unique in world history because throughout America's wars, the vast majority of its soldiers and seaman were citizens who had to be mobilized due to some new threat rather than a standing imperial army devoted to international conquest or domestic patrolling. Today, America's valiant and technologically sophisticated military is relatively small in size as a percentage of the population: approximately 1.4 million active duty and 800,000+ reservists (Reserves and National Guard).

Why bring up DIME in a book on Christian just war statecraft? I mention DIME as one way to recognize that there are nearly unlimited vocations to which Christians are called to serve to promote peace and security. The elements of diplomacy, information, military preparedness, and economics intersect and strengthen one another: all four work together toward the ultimate goal of security and peace. Not only should we pray for our leaders in far-off Washington, DC, London, or other capitals, but we should recognize the God-ordained calling to advance peace for all the citizens working in these four arenas. Our world is better for these public servants, and we are in particular need of highly skilled Christian statesmen, diplomats, humanitarians, warriors, and other experts.

A second, complementary framework for thinking about the different ways that Christians can work to promote peace is to think about roles across the spectrum of insecurity. Western military doctrine speaks of multiple phases of war. To summarize: In the prewar, state governments attempt to dissuade and deter potential threats. This may become a period of heightened insecurity, perhaps a humanitarian crisis or rising tensions due to increased political belligerence. At times, this instability accelerates to hot war. Long before the war ends, experts should be negotiating and preparing for the postwar phase, gearing up for postwar recovery, considering a new political infrastructure of order and justice, and the like. The objective of the late- and postconflict phase is to avoid the instability that led to war in the first place. The ultimate goal is to establish a better state of peace.

There are Christians who are called to serve in every phase of conflict. We need Christian diplomats who are working to soften disagreements, forge compromises, and even issue stern warnings. In some cases, these are "Track Two" diplomats, a term given to private sector individuals, including religious or business leaders, who serve as private intermediaries to their own governments or their counterparts in other countries, such as in the case of Community Sant'Egidio's work in Mozambique.

In areas where there is a humanitarian crisis, there are almost always Christians working via relief organizations such as World Vision, Samaritan's Purse, and Operation Blessing. They are there before the UN and Western governments arrive, and the faith-based humanitarians will be there long after the military departs. Some of these humanitarians work for government or intergovernmental agencies such as USAID or the UN High Commissioner for Refugees.

When the bullets start to fly, we need principled Christians to be involved in the halls of power making decisions, like Daniel and Joseph in the Old Testament, and we need principled Christians operating in the military, adhering to the moral principles of just war thinking. At war's end, Christians will continue to serve on the ground to ameliorate suffering, from the reconstruction of infrastructure to trauma and grief counseling to veterans' care. We desperately need Christians to bring their wisdom to negotiating the new political order, establishing reasonable justice, and seeking long-term conciliation.

Earlier in this chapter we considered forgiveness and conciliation. Forgiveness is not easy to achieve between millions of people via their governments. However, there are a number of areas where Christians can work for conciliation at the individual level. In the Christian church, pastors and spiritual leaders must preach that even in times of war, there is no place in the Christian heart for hatred. We fight for our country, for what is right, for our allies, to preserve human life and property, and for the vindication of rights. We do not fight for revenge, or out of lust, hatred, or greed.

It is not only the warriors who need this message. It is especially needed for their spouses, children, and parents. It is needed for the fallen and the wounded. Pastors have a responsibility for leading their congregations through reflection, healing, and forgiveness.

Other Christians will serve in ministries of healing and concilia-tion. Some of this is the healing of the body, through the medical arts and sciences, whether triaging patients on the margins of battlefields or managing longer-term care and recovery of veterans at home. Many wounds are hidden, but just as lethal, and we need Christian counselors, psychiatrists, and psychologists to serve as agents of heal-ing for trauma, PTSD, moral injury, and moral bruising.[19]

In sum, there is no opt-out option for the people who call them-selves Christ-followers. Christians are called to serve in the time and place where God has put them and utilize the skills and talents he has given them. Whether preparing the hearts of the local church for how to prayerfully respond to injustice and violence, caring for the destitute in a hospital in Africa, fighting on the front lines to stop a genocide in the Middle East, negotiating a just peace treaty in Europe, protecting one's locale from criminals and terrorists, or serving the psychiatric needs of veterans on the home front, there are many roles in which Christians are called to serve across the various phases of conflict. These are virtuous callings.

Pastors can lift up the work of such professionals. Congregations can join in prayer for warriors, politicians, diplomats, and aid workers who are responding—at their own peril—to the geopolitical hazards of fallen humanity. We live in a sinful and insecure world. Some Chris-tians are called to work in situations of violence and instability to help others in dire situations, including before, during, and at the end of conflicts. All Christians are called to pray, and all can contribute to making our society a place that shapes the character of tomorrow's just warriors. This is why Christian thinking, and action, are needed in times of war and peace.

Notes

Chapter 1 Just War Statecraft

1. C. S. Lewis, *Mere Christianity* (New York: HarperOne, 2001), 32.

2. This 1939 address became "Learning in Wartime," later published in C. S. Lewis, *The Weight of Glory, and Other Addresses* (New York: HarperOne, 2001), 47–63. For the quotation, see p. 49.

3. C. S. Lewis, "Why I Am Not a Pacifist," in *The Weight of Glory, and Other Addresses* (New York: HarperOne, 2001), 79 (italics added).

4. Thomas Aquinas, *Summa Theologica* II-II, q. 29.

5. Lewis, "Why I Am Not a Pacifist," 86.

6. Augustine, *Contra Faustum* 23–33, trans. by Richard Stothert, in vol. 4 of *The Nicene and Post-Nicene Fathers*, Series 1, ed. Philip Schaff (1887; repr., Peabody, MA: Hendrickson, 1994), available at https://ccel.org/ccel/schaff/npnf104/npnf104.iv.ix.xxv.html.

7. See the quotation of Augustine in Thomas Aquinas, *Summa Theologica* II-II, q. 40.

8. Franklin Delano Roosevelt, "Quarantine Speech" (Chicago, October 5, 1937), available at https://wwnorton.com/college/history/archive/resources/documents/ch29_03.htm. The speech seemed to be calling for economic sanctions rather than US involvement in either the Spanish Civil War or Japan's invasion of China.

9. Lewis, "Why I Am Not a Pacifist," 62.

Chapter 2 Theological Foundations of Just War Statecraft

1. The New Testament lays out a model for the church's governance (Acts 6:1–6; 1 Cor. 12:28; 1 Tim. 3:1–13), its sustainability (Matt. 6:1–4; Mark 12:41–44; cf. Mal. 3:10–12), and the resolution of its disputes (Matt. 18:15–17; 1 Cor. 5:11; Titus 3:10).

2. Two outstanding resources on vocation and stewardship are Paul Helm, *The Callings: The Gospel in the World* (Edinburgh: Banner of Truth, 1987) and J. Daryl

Charles, *Wisdom and Work: Theological Reflections on Human Labor from Eccle-siastes* (Eugene, OR: Cascade, 2021).

3. Charles Bugg, "Stewardship," in *Holman Bible Dictionary*, ed. Trent Butler (Nashville: Holman, 1991), available at https://www.studylight.org/dictionaries/eng /hbd/s/stewardship.html.

4. "What Is Biblical Stewardship?," Christian Stewardship Network, October 21, 2020, https://www.christianstewardshipnetwork.com/blog/what-is-biblical-steward ship.

5. This formulation derives directly from Augustine, as recorded in Aquinas's *Summa Theologica* II-II, q. 40.

6. We will return to these elements in chap. 6.

Chapter 3 Historical Overview of the Christian Just War Tradition

1. Suzanne Collins, *The Hunger Games* (New York: Scholastic Press, 2008), 18.

2. Thomas Aquinas, *Summa Theologica* II-II, q. 40, art. 1, obj. 4 [answer].

3. Charles reports on the historical context and position of early church fathers such as Tertullian (who thought that political and military service were forms of pagan sacrifice) and Origen—both of whom admit that Christians were serving in the Roman military. J. Daryl Charles, "Presumption against War or Presumption against Injustice? The Just War Tradition Reconsidered," *Journal of Church and State* 48, no. 3 (Fall 2005): 335–69. Charles points out that even the Quaker pacifist Roland Bainton suggests that the occupation of soldiering was likely not completely off-limits to early Christians. See Bainton, *Christian Attitudes toward War and Peace* (New York: Abingdon, 1960), 66, 81.

4. C. S. Lewis, *The Weight of Glory, and Other Addresses* (New York: Harper-One, 2001), 87.

5. Frederick H. Russell discusses how the limited teaching of Christ on violence ultimately resulted in early church leaders, such as Origen and later Ambrose and Augustine, having to define a Christian position on military service, allegiance to the state, and war in general. See his *The Just War in the Middle Ages* (Cambridge: Cambridge University Press, 1975), chap. 2.

6. Adrian Goldsworthy, *Pax Romana: War, Peace, and Conquest in the Roman World* (New Haven: Yale University Press, 2016), 191.

7. For a look at historical and contemporary Christian pacifism from its most famous contemporary defender, see John Howard Yoder, *The Original Revolution: Essays on Christian Pacifism*, Christian Peace Shelf Series (Philadelphia: Herald Press, 2003). For a history of the application of pacifism in American politics, see Theron F. Schlabach and Richard T. Hughes, eds., *Proclaim Peace: Christian Pacifism from Unexpected Quarters* (Urbana: University of Illinois Press, 1997).

8. Michael Ott, "Thundering Legion," in *The Catholic Encyclopedia*, vol. 14 (New York: Robert Appleton Company, 1912), available at http://www.newadvent .org/cathen/14711b.htm.

9. The best resource for pastors and scholars on these issues is Timothy Demy and J. Daryl Charles, *War, Peace, and Christianity: Questions and Answers from a Christian Perspective* (Wheaton: Crossway, 2010). For material on Origen, Tertullian, and other church fathers, see pp. 113–20.

10. For a brief introduction to this entire controversy, see James Turner Johnson, "Just War, as It Was and Is," *First Things* 149 (January 2005): 19.

11. Augustine wrote letters to a Roman military leader named Boniface as well as to an ecclesiastical figure named Boniface. The two should not be confused.

12. Augustine, *Letters* 189.5, in *Nicene and Post-Nicene Fathers of the Christian Church*, 1st series, ed. Philip Schaff, vol. 1, *Confessions and Letters of St. Augustine* (New York: Christian Literature, 1886), available at http://www.ccel.org/ccel/schaff /npnf101.vii.1.CLXXXIX.html?highlight=augustine,letter,boniface,war#fna_vii .1.CLXXXIX-p3.2.

13. Augustine's *The City of God* [*De civitate Dei*] is his famous treatise contrasting the *civitas Dei* and the *civitas terrena*. However, we gather much of his just war thinking from his voluminous correspondence, such as *To Publicola* and *To Marcellinus*. Many of these letters are available in classic compilations from the Catholic University of America (CUA) Press as well as in a new series by New City Press.

14. Augustine, *City of God* 19.12 in *Nicene and Post-Nicene Fathers*, 1st series, vol. 2, ed. Philip Schaff, trans. Marcus Dods (New York: Christian Literature, 1886).

15. Contemporary Roman Catholic public intellectual George Weigel has written extensively on this topic, including an entire book on the tranquility of order. For a brief overview of his views on Augustine and this topic, see his speech on accepting the Peace Prize of the Universal Peace Project: George Weigel, "What 'Peace' Means Today," *National Review Online*, October 13, 2016, https://www.nationalreview.com /2016/10/what-peace-means-moral-truth-starting-point/.

16. This famous quote from Augustine is referred to in Thomas Aquinas, *Summa Theologica* II-II, q. 40, 2nd ed., trans. Fathers of the English Dominican Province (London: Burns, Oates, & Washburne, 1920–35), available at https://www.newadvent .org/summa/3040.htm.

17. Roger Epp, "The Augustinian Moment in International Politics," International Politics Research Papers 10 (Aberystwyth, UK: Department of International Politics, University College of Wales, 1991).

18. Augustine, *City of God* 19.12.

19. Thomas Aquinas, *Summa Theologica* II-II, q. 40.

20. Thomas Aquinas, *Summa Theologica* II-II, q. 40.

21. Thomas Aquinas, *Summa Theologica* II-II, q. 40.

22. Thomas Aquinas, *Summa Theologica* II-II, q. 40.

23. Thomas Aquinas, *Summa Theologica* II-II, q. 40.

24. Quoted in Richard Shelly Hartigan, "Francesco de Vitoria and Civilian Immunity," *Political Theory* 1, no. 1 (1973): 83. This discussion can be found in Vitoria's work, *De Indis et de iure Belli Reflectiones*, ed. Ernest Nys, trans. J. P. Bate (New York: Oceana / Wildy and Sons, 1964), 449.

25. There is a second strain of pacifism, "nonviolent action," that has roots outside of Christianity in the social movement started by Gandhi. There is no historical evidence of pre-twentieth-century carefully planned Christian nonviolent resistance strategies such as those led by Gandhi and Martin Luther King Jr.'s "nonviolent *direct* action" (the latter's term). Martin Luther King Jr. brought Christian theological elements of witness, neighbor-love, and especially consideration of one's own motivations to classic civil disobedience techniques.

26. The classic statement of the Anabaptist tradition (the Schleitheim Confession) can be found at http://www.anabaptists.org/history/the-schleitheim-confession.html. It is noteworthy that classical Baptists have not accepted this Anabaptist position. In fact, in 1524 the five Baptist churches of London publicly dismissed the Anabaptist position. Unfortunately, few of today's so-called pacifists have grappled with its teaching.

27. Dietrich Bonhoeffer, *Life Together* (San Francisco: Harper & Row, 1954), 64.

28. Quoted in William J. Bouwsma, *John Calvin: A Sixteenth Century Portrait* (New York: Oxford University Press), 60–61.

29. John Knox, *The First Blast of the Trumpet against the Monstrous Regiment of Women*, in *The Works of John Knox*, ed. David Laing, 6 vols. (1846; repr., New York: AMS Press, 1966), 4:429–540, available at https://www.gutenberg.org/files/9660/9660 -h/9660-h.htm. Other influential Reformed authors include Christopher Goodman, *How Superior Power Ought to Be Obeyed*, ed. Charles H. McIlwain (1558; repr., New York: Columbia University Press, 1931); and George Buchanon, *A Dialogue on the Law of Kingship Among the Scots*, ed. Roger A. Mason and Martin S. Smith (1579; repr., Burlington, VT: Ashgate, 2004). In the Netherlands, the most important Reformed figure was Johannes Althusius, a notable apologist for Dutch revolt against the Spanish Emperor Phillip II. See *The Politics of Johannes Althusius: An Abridged Translation of the Third Edition* [1614] *of Politica Methodice digesta atque exemplis saris et profanis illustrata*, trans. with an introduction by Frederick S. Carney, preface by Carl J. Friedrich (Boston: Beacon, 1964).

30. Thomas Aquinas, *On Kingship* 1.6.48, trans. Gerald B. Phelan (Toronto: Pontifical Institute for Mediaeval Studies, 1982).

31. Thomas Aquinas, *2 Sentences* 44.2.2, quoted in William Saunders, "Does the Church Condone Tyrannicide?," Catholic Education Resource Center, https://www .catholiceducation.org/en/culture/catholic-contributions/does-the-church-condone -tyrannicide.html. Saunders outlines Thomas's argument for tyrannicide:

> A tyrant by usurpation has illegitimately seized power and, therefore, is a criminal. When there are no other means available of ridding the community of the tyrant, the community may kill him. According to St. Thomas, the legitimate authority may condemn him to death using the normal course of law. However, if the normal course of law is not available (due to the actions of the tyrant), then the legitimate authority can proceed "informally" to condemn the tyrant and even grant individuals a mandate to execute the tyrant. A private citizen who takes the life of a tyrant acts with public authority in the same way that a soldier does in war. The key conditions for a justifiable act of tyrannicide in this case include that the killing be necessary to end the usurpation and restore legitimate authority; that there is no higher authority available that is able and willing to depose the usurper; and that there is no probability that the tyrannicide will result in even greater evil than allowing the usurper to remain in power.

32. John Calvin, *Institutes of the Christian Religion* 4.20.31, ed. John T. McNeill, trans. Ford Lewis Battles (Philadelphia: Westminster, 1960).

33. Pope John Paul's speech is excerpted in James Turner Johnson, *Morality and Contemporary Warfare* (New Haven: Yale University Press, 2001), 91.

34. US Conference of Catholic Bishops, *The Harvest of Justice Is Sown in Peace* (Washington, DC: US Conference of Catholic Bishops, 1993), https://www.usccb.org

/resources/harvest-justice-sown-peace. Also see the brief statement by the National Association of Evangelicals, citing just war principles and the sometime need for humanitarian intervention: *For the Health of the Nation* (2004), https://www.nae .org/for-the-health-of-the-nation-publication/.

35. US Conference of Catholic Bishops, *Harvest of Justice Is Sown in Peace*.

36. Jean Bethke Elshtain, "Just War as an Ethics of Responsibility," in *Ethics beyond War's End*, ed. Eric Patterson (Washington, DC: Georgetown University Press, 2012).

37. J. Daryl Charles, "The Ethics of Humanitarian Intervention (2010)," in *Power Politics and Moral Order*, ed. Eric Patterson and Robert Joustra (Eugene, OR: Cascade, 2022), 257–70.

38. Charles, "Ethics of Humanitarian Intervention," 77–78.

39. See Reinhold Niebuhr, "An Open Letter to Richard Roberts," *Christianity and Society* 5 (Summer 1940): 30–33. This argument is updated in thoughtful chapters by Paul Ramsey, William V. O'Brien, and Jean Bethke Elshtain published in *Just War Theory*, ed. Jean Bethke Elshtain (New York: New York University Press, 1992).

40. C. S. Lewis, "Why I Am Not a Pacifist," in *The Weight of Glory, and Other Addresses* (New York: HarperOne, 2001), 71.

41. See Niebuhr, "Open Letter to Richard Roberts."

42. See Niebuhr, "Open Letter to Richard Roberts."

43. Reinhold Niebuhr, *Why the Christian Church Is Not Pacifist* [pamphlet] (London: Student Christian Movement Press, 1940).

Chapter 4 Morality and Contemporary Warfare

1. Martin Luther King Jr., *Letter from Birmingham Jail* (April 16, 1963). King's letter was also published as part of an article in the same year, "The Negro Is Your Brother," *Atlantic Monthly*, August 1963, 78–88.

2. King, *Letter from Birmingham Jail*.

3. King, *Letter from Birmingham Jail*.

4. King, *Letter from Birmingham Jail*.

5. Martin Luther King Jr., "Martin Luther King Jr. on Just and Unjust Laws: Excerpts from a Letter to Fellow Clergymen Written from Birmingham City Jail, April 16, 1963," available at https://www.jfklibrary.org/sites/default/files/2020-04 /Birmingham%20Letter%20Excerpts%20for%20Activity.pdf.

6. King, *Letter from Birmingham Jail*.

7. King, *Letter from Birmingham Jail*.

8. King, *Letter from Birmingham Jail*.

9. King, *Letter from Birmingham Jail*.

10. "German Military Oaths," Holocaust Encyclopedia, United States Holocaust Memorial Museum, https://encyclopedia.ushmm.org/content/en/article/german-mil itary-oaths.

11. "The German Churches and the Nazi State," Holocaust Encyclopedia, United States Holocaust Memorial Museum, https://encyclopedia.ushmm.org/content/en /article/the-german-churches-and-the-nazi-state.

12. Bill Broadway, "The Theology and Martyrdom of Dietrich Bonhoeffer," *Washington Post*, April 8, 1995, https://www.washingtonpost.com/archive/local/1995/04

/08/the-theology-and-martydrom-of-dietrich-bonhoeffer/d0a89f70-2fd8-4ca6-bc51
-90b4c4cc6fec/.

13. Dietrich Bonhoeffer, *Life Together* (San Francisco: Harper & Row, 1954), 64.

14. The classic statement of this is derived from the Third Geneva Convention, article 4, on prisoners of war. "Prisoners of war, in the sense of the present Convention, are persons belonging to one of the following categories, who have fallen into the power of the enemy: (1) Members of the armed forces of a Party to the conflict, as well as members of militias or volunteer corps forming part of such armed forces. (2) Members of other militias and members of other volunteer corps, including those of organized resistance movements, belonging to a Party to the conflict and operating in or outside their own territory, even if this territory is occupied, provided that such militias or volunteer corps, including such organized resistance movements, fulfil the following conditions: (a) that of being commanded by a person responsible for his subordinates; (b) that of having a fixed distinctive sign recognizable at a distance; (c) that of carrying arms openly; (d) that of conducting their operations in accordance with the laws and customs of war." "Convention (III) Relative to the Treatment of Prisoners of War. Geneva, 12 August 1949," International Humanitarian Law Databases, https://ihl-databases.icrc.org/en/ihl-treaties/gciii-1949.

15. See the quoted statement under A.(2)(a) in the quotation of "Convention (III) Relative to the Treatment of Prisoners of War," n. 12.

16. Cristina Rojas and Judy Meltzer, eds., *Elusive Peace: International, National, and Local Dimensions of Conflict in Colombia* (New York: Palgrave Macmillan, 2005); Virginia M. Bouvier, ed., *Colombia: Building Peace in a Time of War* (Washington, DC: United States Institute of Peace Press, 2009).

17. See Steven M. Dworetz, *The Unvarnished Doctrine: Locke, Liberalism and the American Revolution* (Durham, NC: Duke University Press, 1990), 156: "The clergy did not treat St. Paul as a radical simply as a matter of Revolutionary exigency. Jonathan Mayhew in 1750, and Samuel West in 1776, offered the same 'liberal' interpretation of Romans 13. Even before Mayhew this interpretation appeared in a number of pamphlets and sermons. . . . The 'liberal' reading of Romans 13 was not, in fact, an American innovation. Quentin Skinner traces the prototype to John Colet, a fifteenth century English humanist."

18. Samuel West, "On the Right to Rebel against Governors" (Boston, 1776), in *American Political Writing during the Founding Era: 1760–1785*, ed. Charles S. Hyneman and Donald L. Lutz, vols. 1 and 2 (Indianapolis: Liberty Fund, 1983), 412.

19. John Adams on Mayhew as cited in Eric Patterson, "Jonathan Mayhew: Colonial Pastor against Tyranny," *Providence*, October 8, 2020, https://providencemag.com/2020/10/jonathan-mayhew-colonial-pastor-against-tyranny/#_ednref1.

20. Jonathan Mayhew, *Discourse concerning Unlimited Submission and Non-Resistance to Higher Authorities* [sermon published in 1750], quoted in Patterson, "Jonathan Mayhew." Mayhew's sermon is available at http://nationalhumanitiescenter.org/pds/becomingamer/american/text5/mayhewsubmission.pdf.

21. Mayhew, *Discourse concerning Unlimited Submission*, quoted in Patterson, "Jonathan Mayhew."

22. Mayhew, *Discourse concerning Unlimited Submission*, quoted in Patterson, "Jonathan Mayhew."

23. *Declaration of the United Colonies on the Causes and Necessities of Taking Up Arms*, issued by the Continental Congress in July 1775. The entire declaration can be found through the Avalon Project, Yale Law School, http://avalon.law.yale .edu/18th_century/arms.asp.

24. *Declaration of the United Colonies on the Causes and Necessities of Taking Up Arms*.

25. See, e.g., Mayhew, *Discourse concerning Unlimited Submission*, quoted in Patterson, "Jonathan Mayhew"; see also Dworetz, *Unvarnished Doctrine*.

26. *Declaration of the United Colonies on the Causes and Necessities of Taking Up Arms*.

27. *Declaration of the United Colonies on the Causes and Necessities of Taking Up Arms*. Bullets added and formatting modified.

28. *Declaration of the United Colonies on the Causes and Necessities of Taking Up Arms*.

29. *Declaration of the United Colonies on the Causes and Necessities of Taking Up Arms*.

30. *Declaration of the United Colonies on the Causes and Necessities of Taking Up Arms*.

31. *Declaration of the United Colonies on the Causes and Necessities of Taking Up Arms*.

Chapter 5 The Motivations and Characteristics of Just Warriors

1. These quotes are taken from the Sergeant York Patriotic Foundation website, https://sgtyork.org/.

2. Mother Teresa, "Acceptance Speech" (Nobel Peace Prize acceptance speech, University of Oslo, Norway, December 10, 1979), https://www.nobelprize.org/prizes /peace/1979/teresa/acceptance-speech/.

3. Pat Tillman quote taken from Pat Tillman Foundation website, https://pattillman foundation.org/.

4. C. S. Lewis, *The Four Loves* (New York: HarperOne, 2017), 225.

5. Lewis, *Four Loves*, 225–28.

6. Lewis, *Four Loves*, 228.

7. Samuel Francis Smith, "My Country, 'Tis of Thee" (ca. 1861). See "My Country 'Tis of Thee," Library of Congress, 2002, https://loc.gov/item/ihas.200000012.

8. *Star Trek: The Wrath of Khan*, directed by Nicholas Meyer (Hollywood, CA: Paramount Pictures, 1982).

9. That radio speech became C. S. Lewis, "Forgiveness," chap. 7 in *Mere Christianity* (New York: HarperOne, 2001), 115.

10. Lewis, "Forgiveness," 116–17.

11. Lewis, "Forgiveness," 116–17.

12. Lewis, "Forgiveness," 116–17.

13. *Star Wars: Episode I—The Phantom Menace*, directed by George Lucas (Los Angeles: Twentieth Century Fox, 1999).

14. C. S. Lewis, *Reflections on the Psalms* (New York: Harcourt Brace, 1958), 118.

15. Lewis, *Reflections on the Psalms*, 146.

16. Lewis, *Reflections on the Psalms*, 146.

17. Lewis, *Reflections on the Psalms*, 148.

18. Lewis, *Reflections on the Psalms*, 147.

19. Lewis, *Mere Christianity*, 117.

20. Homer, *The Iliad* 1.1–6, trans. Stanley Lombardo (Indianapolis: Hackett, 1997), available at https://poets.org/poem/iliad-book-i-lines-1-15.

21. See Marc LiVecche, *The Good Kill: Just War and Moral Injury* (New York: Oxford University Press, 2021).

Chapter 6 Ending Wars Well

1. C. S. Lewis, *The Lion, the Witch and the Wardrobe* (New York: Collier, 1970), 177.

2. This model was developed for and appeared in my book *Ending Wars Well: Order, Justice, and Conciliation in Post-Conflict* (New Haven: Yale University Press, 2012).

3. Desmond Tutu and Mpho Tutu, "Desmond Tutu: On Why We Forgive," Daily Good, May 6, 2014, https://www.dailygood.org/story/688/desmond-tutu-on-why-we-forgive-desmond-tutu-and-mpho-tutu/.

4. This version of the passage is taken directly from the community's website, https://www.santegidio.org/pageID/1/langID/en/HOME.html.

5. These quotes have been brought together in a case study of the peace process, "Mozambique: Religious Peacebuilders Broker End to the Civil War," Berkley Center for Religion, Peace & World Affairs, August 1, 2013, https://berkleycenter.georgetown.edu/publications/mozambique-religious-peacebuilders-broker-end-to-civil-war.

6. Abraham Lincoln, "Lincoln's Second Inaugural Address" (Washington, DC, March 4, 1865), available at https://www.nps.gov/linc/learn/historyculture/lincoln-second-inaugural.htm.

7. John George Nicolay and John Hay, *Abraham Lincoln: A History*, vol. 6 (New York: Century, 1890), chap. 15, p. 324. Lincoln wrote this as part of a response to the 1864 general conference of the Methodist Episcopal Church.

8. Abraham Lincoln to George B. Ide, James R. Doolittle, and A. Hubbell, May 30, 1864, in *Collected Works of Abraham Lincoln*, ed. Roy P. Basler, vol. 7, Abraham Lincoln Association (New Brunswick, NJ: Rutgers University Press, 1953), available at https://quod.lib.umich.edu/l/lincoln/lincoln7/1:822.1?rgn=div2;view=fulltext.

9. Abraham Lincoln, Speech at Great Central Sanitary Fair, Philadelphia, Pennsylvania, June 16, 1864, in Basler, *Collected Works of Abraham Lincoln*, available at https://quod.lib.umich.edu/l/lincoln/lincoln7/1:878?rgn=div1;view=fulltext.

10. Abraham Lincoln to Eliza Gurney, September 4, 1864, in Basler, *Collected Works of Abraham Lincoln*, available at https://quod.lib.umich.edu/l/lincoln/lincoln7/1:1171.1?rgn=div2;view=fulltext;q1=Eliza+P.+Gurney.

11. Abraham Lincoln, "President Lincoln's First Message, July 4, 1861," in Edward McPherson, *The Political History of the United States of America, during the Great Rebellion, from November 6, 1860, to July 4, 1864* (Washington, DC: Philip & Solomons, 1865), 126.

12. Abraham Lincoln, Statement to Secretary of War Edwin M. Stanton, February 5, 1864, in Basler, *Collected Works of Abraham Lincoln*, available at https://quod.lib.umich.edu/l/lincoln/lincoln7/1:358.1?rgn=div2;view=fulltext.

13. Thaddeus Stevens, "Reconstruction: Hon. Thaddeus Stevens on the Great Topic of the Hour; An Address Delivered to the Citizens of Lancaster, September 6, 1865," *New York Times*, September 10, 1865, https://www.nytimes.com/1865/09/10/archives/reconstruction-hon-thaddeus-stevens-on-the-great-topic-of-the-hour.html.

14. Woodrow Wilson, "8 January 1918: President Woodrow Wilson's Fourteen Points," available at https://avalon.law.yale.edu/20th_century/wilson14.asp.

15. Woodrow Wilson, "8 January 1918: President Woodrow Wilson's Fourteen Points."

16. C. S. Lewis, *Mere Christianity* (New York: HarperOne, 2001), 119.

17. Abraham Lincoln, "Abraham Lincoln: Second Inaugural Address, March 4, 1865," available at https://sourcebooks.fordham.edu/mod/1865lincoln-aug2.asp.

18. See also chap. 2, under "Just War Principles Rooted in Governance, Calling, and Stewardship."

19. It is beyond the scope of this chapter to go into the nuances of these categories. The best primer from an explicitly Christian perspective is Marc LiVecche's *The Good Kill: Just War and Moral Injury* (Oxford: Oxford University Press, 2021). Post-traumatic stress disorder, recognized by previous generations with terms such as "shell shock," refers to a "broadly defined mental health disorder" emerging from "exposure to . . . or witnessing, a particular kind of traumatic event, typically life threatening and of such intensity that it results in stressors outside the range of human experience." Note that PTSD's stressors are from "outside the sufferer," unlike other mental health problems (e.g., those associated with chemical imbalance). In recent years a different diagnosis, "moral injury," has been used by individuals such as Jonathan Shay and Litz and Maguen (here quoted in LiVecche) to describe the "lasting psychological . . . impact of perpetrating, failing to prevent, or bearing witness to acts that transgress deeply held moral beliefs and expectations." An example might result from a US Marine killing a child in combat, despite the fact that the thirteen-year-old Afghan male was shooting a rifle at the Marine under foggy conditions. LiVecche differentiates moral *injury* from moral *bruising*, the latter a term for times when it is not forgiveness that is needed (no moral wrong was done, though a tragedy occurred) but rather vindication (yes, a tragedy occurred; here are the steps toward coming to terms with something that was entirely not your fault). See LiVecche's excellent discussion of these issues with definitions and citations (21–25).

Suggested Reading

Biggar, Nigel. *In Defence of War*. Oxford: Oxford University Press, 2013.

Capizzi, Joseph E. *Politics, Justice, and War: Christian Governance and the Ethics of Warfare*. Oxford: Oxford University Press, 2015.

Charles, J. Daryl, and Timothy J. Demy. *War, Peace, and Christianity: Questions and Answers from a Just War Perspective*. New York: Crossway, 2010.

Copan, Paul, ed. *War, Peace, and Violence: Four Christian Views*. Downers Grove, IL: InterVarsity, 2022.

Corey, David D., and J. Daryl Charles. *The Just War Tradition: An Introduction*. Wilmington, DE: ISI Books, 2012.

Elshtain, Jean Bethke. *Just War against Terror*. New York: Basic Books, 2003.

Johnson, James Turner. "Just War, as It Was and Is." *First Things* 149 (January 2005): 19.

Lewis, C. S. "Learning in Wartime." In *The Weight of Glory, and Other Addresses*, 47–63. New York: HarperOne, 2001. First published 1949.

———. "Why I Am Not a Pacifist." In *The Weight of Glory, and Other Addresses*, 64–90. New York: HarperOne, 2001. First published 1949.

LiVecche, Marc. *The Good Kill: Just War and Moral Injury*. Oxford: Oxford University Press, 2021.

Patterson, Eric, and J. Daryl Charles, eds. *Just War and Christian Traditions*. Notre Dame, IN: University of Notre Dame Press, 2022.

Patterson, Eric, and Timothy J. Demy, eds. *Philosophers on War*. Newport, RI: Stone Tower Press, 2017.

Patterson, Eric, and Robert Joustra, eds. *Power Politics and Moral Order: Three Generations of Christian Realism*. Eugene, OR: Cascade, 2022.

Pavlischek, Keith J. "Reinhold Niebuhr, Christian Realism, and Just War Theory: A Critique." In *Christianity and Power Politics Today: Christian Realism and Contemporary Political Dilemmas*, edited by Eric Patterson, 53–71. New York: Palgrave Macmillan, 2008.

Providence: A Journal of Christianity and American Foreign Policy. Available at providencemag.org.

Ramsey, Paul. *The Just War: Force and Political Responsibility*. Lanham, MD: Rowman & Littlefield, 2002. First published 1968.

Smith, Bradford. *Brave Rifles: The Theology of War*. Fort Knox, KY: Olivia Kimbrell Press, 2017.

Weigel, George. *Peace and Freedom: Christian Faith, Democracy & the Problem of War*. Washington, DC: Institute on Religion and Democracy, 1983.

Index